Capital Management
for Financial Executives

An Alexander Hamilton Institute Book
Chilton's Better Business Series

Capital Management for Financial Executives

Richard B. Stockton

CHILTON BOOK COMPANY
Radnor, Pennsylvania

The Capman model discussed in the Appendix
is available on disk from the publisher.
The price is $12.95 including postage and handling.
Send check or company purchase order to:
  Chilton Book Company
  Department DK
  Radnor, PA 19089

Copyright © 1984, 1985 by Alexander Hamilton Institute, Inc.
Modern Business Reports, 1501 Broadway, New York, NY 10036
All Rights Reserved
Published in Radnor, Pennsylvania 19089, by Chilton Book Company
Designed by Jean Callan King/Metier Industrial, Inc.
Manufactured in the United States of America

Library of Congress Cataloging in Publication Data
Stockton, Richard B.
    Capital management for financial executives.
    (Chilton's better business series)
    "An Alexander Hamilton Institute book."
    Includes index.
    1. Business enterprises—Finance—Case studies.
2. Capital investments—Case studies. I. Title.
II. Series.
HG4015.5.S76 1985   658.1'52   84-72636
ISBN 0-8019-7620-0 *hardcover*
ISBN 0-8019-7632-4 *paperback*

Chilton's Better Business Series

1 2 3 4 5 6 7 8 9 0   3 2 1 0 9 8 7 6 5

Contents

List of Figures

I

Role of Capital and Finance

The decisions that top executives make about how to use capital extend far beyond their own companies. For instance, their decisions affect:

- *the owners of the company*, through profits realized on invested capital;
- *other competing companies*, and their owners, as the result of decisions on capacity, new products, new markets, prices and the like;
- *the entire economy*, since ultimately capital seeks industries and companies where it will receive better rates of return.

The responsibility of management to the owners of companies for effectively deploying capital is especially significant. First, the owners have a right to expect a fair rate of return on the capital they have invested. Second, if executives do satisfy the owners, then they are certain to be able to fulfill their responsibilities to employees, customers, suppliers and the community.

THE ROLES OF FINANCE AND CONTROL/ACCOUNTING

Today the concept of finance is broader than simply obtaining long-term funds. Now finance is heavily involved in the measurement, control, evaluation, and planning of business results.

The senior financial manager may be in a finance, accounting, controller's, or treasurer's department. Figure 1 illustrates the differ-

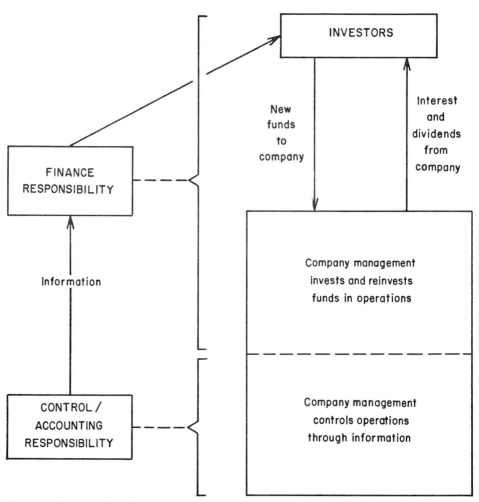

Figure 1. Relationship between finance and control/accounting

ences between the finance and the control/accounting functions as well as how they relate.

Finance is concerned with the investor (who may not be a company manager), and the management of the money that flows to, through, and out of the company. Control/accounting, on the other hand, provides the information on the financial condition of the company. Obviously, there must be a close working relationship between the finance and control/accounting functions.

Investors provide funds to the company and expect to receive dividends and interest from the company. Management of the company, assisted by the finance function, manage the funds received by investing and reinvesting them in operations. Control/accounting, on the other hand, provides the information necessary to control operations, feeds information to finance which has the dual responsibilities of acting on the information, and keeping the investors informed.

THE CHALLENGE OF MANAGING CAPITAL

Raising new capital to meet the growing needs of business has become more difficult and complex in recent years. An unstable environment, major changes in life-styles, consumer tastes, and technology require greater management attention.

Governments, through regulation, taxation, and growth, are increasing their impacts on business and the availability of capital. They are also the engines of inflation.

These developments cause top executives to ask complex questions such as:

- How much can I really afford to spend on capital replacement and expansion?
- How will the expenditures be financed?
- How does the cost of the financing affect the decision on how much to spend?
- If I don't spend to replace or expand facilities, how will my profits and return on investment be affected?
- What are my capital costs? Are they increasing or decreasing?

- How can I set profit goals for the company or a division?
- Is my company worth more this year than last?
- What is the outlook for next year?
- How are my decisions affecting the value of the company?

This report will reveal financial principles and analytical techniques that can be used to answer these and other tough questions.

Profitability and return on investment are the bases for making correct decisions on capital management. The supply of capital is limited. Its cost has been increasing. The success, or even survival of a company today, depends on how well its executives manage it.

THE ROLE OF THE MANAGER OF FINANCE

Where and how capital is obtained is not within the scope of this book. But when a company can demonstrate solid profit growth and attractive returns on invested capital, raising capital becomes much easier. The productive use of capital attracts investment. The financial techniques described in this report lead to improved results.

While decisions on capital investment and financing are made by top management, the burden for producing the necessary information falls on the senior finance manager in the company. This responsibility provides him or her with an opportunity to make a meaningful and significant contribution. It is also true that some understanding of finance by all managers can lead to more efficient use of capital and to better teamwork.

FINANCIAL OBJECTIVES

Financial management involves two major objectives:

1. Adequate cash flow for operating and investment purposes.
2. Operations as profitable as possible.

These objectives are inseparable. Cash flow is linked to profit levels. The more profitable the operation is, the more cash will be available for investment and the easier it will be to attract additional capital for expansion. This book deals extensively with cash flow and profit levels in relation to the capital invested.

FUNDAMENTALS ARE APPLICABLE TO ALL SIZES OF BUSINESS

The principles of capital management are applicable to companies of all sizes, whether publicly or privately owned. Often the investors, owners and top managers in small companies are the same persons. They often feel free from external pressures in setting profit goals and making investment decisions.This perception is a trap and can prove fatal.

For instance, the owner/manager of a small business may choose to operate at low profit levels or even at a loss. There are practical limits to such choices dictated by the supply and cost of capital invested. Capital can be attracted only by a fair rate of return, and the owner/ manager will in time exhaust his own supply of capital. Ultimately he must change to an acceptable level of profitability or go out of business. Therefore, the principles of capital management apply to all.

FINANCIAL ANALYSIS

Managers use financial analysis to determine whether operations are meeting financial expectations. Investors use it to judge the investment value of the company.

The following Sections describe a typical, but hypothetical, manufacturing company for analysis from the viewpoints of its managers and investors. The best way to illustrate how finance can be used as a working tool is by examining a going concern and showing how financial information can be used to achieve its objectives.

II

Effective Approaches to Financial Statement Analysis

The balance sheet, the statement of income, and the statement of changes in financial position are major sources of factual information that should be used to control, plan and make decisions. These statements show a company's financial position only on the statement date. However, analyzing the latest financial statements and comparing them to prior periods uncovers strengths, weaknesses, and trends that will affect future performance.

It is a basic responsibility of the financial manager and top executives to recognize and interpret changes and trends affecting the profitability and financial integrity of the company. When the financial manager analyzes the statements regularly, he can identify developing problems that may keep actual results from reaching expectations. He can then provide more effective financial guidelines to the company's operating managers. Their common objective is to earn a satisfactory return on the capital invested.

A CASE STUDY OF STATEMENT ANALYSIS

The Noxton Manufacturing Company is a hypothetical but typical medium-sized company. C.M. Jones has just been hired as director of finance, a new position reporting directly to the president. Jones decides, as one of his first tasks, to analyze Noxton's statements to determine how effectively the company's capital is being managed and to identify the areas for improvement.

Noxton has grown steadily since it was founded 15 years ago. It produces electrical components, sophisticated controls, and other industrial products for sale to contractors and manufacturers. The company produces quality products and is highly regarded by its customers and creditors. The two original owners decided to sell stock to the public eight years ago and sold 80 percent of their shares. They remain with the company as chairman of the board and president. Noxton has approximately 1,100 stockholders.

The company has a number of competitors, some of whom are considerably larger. Noxton estimates its share of the market for its products is 8 percent with little change over the past few years. Customers are sophisticated buyers and price is of great importance. Because of its size, management believes it must adjust to its competitors' prices. Quality and dependability of delivery schedules are key selling points.

The company's plant and equipment are relatively new and efficient. The work force is stable. There are no contingent liabilities that would have a material adverse effect. In summary, the company appears to be in reasonably good condition.

PREPARATION FOR ANALYSIS

The audited financial statements for Noxton for fiscal years 19X6 and 19X5 are shown in Figures 2 and 3. The explanatory notes state that the company uses the LIFO method to value inventory and straight line depreciation for book purposes. There are no major nonrecurring items affecting either the 19X6 or 19X5 results which would require adjustment to make results comparable with those of prior years. Jones, of course, would not hesitate to make adjustments in order to improve

THE NOXTON MANUFACTURING COMPANY
BALANCE SHEET (as of June 30)
(000 omitted)

Assets	19X6	19X5
Current assets		
Cash	$ 190	$ 200
Certificates of deposit	700	700
Accounts receivable (net)	1,472	1,220
Inventories:		
Finished goods	800	950
Work in process	3,000	2,482
Purchased materials	500	360
Total inventories	4,300	3,792
Prepaid expenses	40	40
Total current assets	6,702	5,952
Property, plant & equipment, at cost		
Land	450	450
Buildings	2,500	2,500
Machinery & equipment	2,400	2,368
	5,350	5,318
Less accumulated depreciation	1,557	1,400
Net property, plant & equipment	3,793	3,918
Other assets	75	75
Total assets	$10,570	$ 9,945

Liabilities and Stockholders' Equity	19X6	19X5
Current liabilities		
Accounts payable	$ 1,160	$ 980
Notes payable	600	500
Income taxes payable	100	70
Other expenses	430	390
Total current liabilities	2,290	1,940
Long-term debt, 8% notes	2,500	2,500
Deferred income taxes	300	250
Total liabilities	5,090	4,690

Figure 2. The balance sheet

THE NOXTON MANUFACTURING COMPANY
BALANCE SHEET (as of June 30), *continued*
(000 omitted)

Liabilities and Stockholders' Equity	19X6	19X5
Stockholders' equity		
Preferred stock, 5% cumulative, $100 par value each; authorized, 10,000 shares; issued and outstanding, none	—	—
Common stock, $1 par value each; authorized— 1,000,000 shares; issued and outstanding— 700,000 shares	700	700
Capital surplus	1,400	1,400
Retained earnings	3,380	3,155
Total stockholders' equity	5,480	5,255
Total liabilities and stockholders' equity	$10,570	$ 9,945

Figure 2. Continued

comparability of information to other companies or to prior years' results. It is the *accountant's* job to see that the financial statements accurately reflect the results for the year. It is Jones' job as an analyst to determine whether the results as reported are truly representative of the period in terms of earning capability.

Jones has copies of prior annual reports and reads the notes and comments to insure they are consistent with 19X6 and 19X5. He plans to use selected information for years 19X4, 19X3 and 19X2 to prepare a key ratio analysis for a five-year period. He knows that the industry experienced a modest slowdown in activity during the latter part of 19X2 and early 19X3.

ANALYZING THE STATEMENT OF INCOME

The income statement shows that sales and net income in 19X6 exceeded 19X5 by 12.3 and 14.8 percent, respectively. While it appears that 19X6 was a good year, Jones prepares the worksheet shown in Figure 4 to compare in percentage form certain figures from the statement. By re-

THE NOXTON MANUFACTURING COMPANY
(Year ended June 30)
(000 omitted)

Statement of Income and Retained Earnings	19X6	19X5
Sales	$14,415	$12,836
Cost of sales	11,775	10,440
Selling and shipping expenses	725	670
Administrative and general expenses	600	530
	13,100	11,640
Operating income	1,315	1,196
Interest and other income	35	40
Interest and other expense	(250)	(260)
Income before income taxes	1,100	976
Provision for income taxes	525	475
Net income	575	501
Retained earnings at beginning of year	3,155	3,004
Cash dividends ($.50 per share)	(350)	(350)
Retained earnings at end of year	$ 3,380	$ 3,155
Net income per share of common stock	$ .82	$ .72

Statement of Changes in Financial Position	19X6	19X5
Sources of funds		
Operations		
Net income	$ 575	$ 501
Depreciation	325	300
Deferred tax	50	25
	950	826
Reductions (additions to) other assets	—	(10)
	950	816
Application of funds		
Additions to property, plant & equipment	200	250
Dividends paid	350	350
	550	600
Increase in working capital	$ 400	$ 216

Figure 3. Statements of income and changes in financial position

THE NOXTON MANUFACTURING COMPANY
(Year ended June 30), *continued*
(000 omitted)

Statement of Changes in Financial Position	19X6	19X5
Changes in components of working capital		
Increases (decreases) in current assets		
Cash	(10)	25
Certificates of deposit	—	(80)
Receivables	252	180
Inventories	508	401
	750	526
Increases (decreases) current liabilities		
Accounts payable	180	170
Notes payable	100	—
Accrued expenses	70	140
	350	310
Increase in working capital	$ 400	$ 216

Figure 3. Continued

ducing these figures to their respective percentages of sales, and comparing them to each other, the financial manager spots changes quickly and gets a clearer picture of actual performance.

For example, Jones notes that operating income of $1,315,000 for 19X6 as shown on the income statement is higher than the $1,196,000 achieved in 19X5. However, when he compares the percentage of operating income to sales, he learns that it is 9.1 percent in 19X6 versus 9.3 percent in 19X5. It appears that operating performance has declined and that the improvement in 19X6's net income was attributable in part to lower nonoperating expenses such as lower interest expense as well as a slightly lower income tax provision. Adjusting for these nonoperating factors he determines that the *net income growth* in 19X6 was nearer to 12 percent than the 14.8 percent that comparison of the two net income figures reveals.

Because cost of sales is such a significant factor in Noxton's profitability, failure to recover these increasing costs can have a severe effect

| | From Income Statement | | Percentages of Sales | |
	19X6	19X5	19X6	19X5
Sales	$14,415	$12,836	100.0%	100.0%
Cost of sales	11,775	10,440	81.7	81.4
Other operating costs	1,325	1,200	9.2	9.3
Operating income	1,315	1,196	9.1	9.3
Other income & other expenses (net)	(215)	(220)	1.5	1.7
Income before taxes	1,100	976	7.6	7.6
Provision for income taxes	525	475	3.6	3.7
Net income	$ 575	$ 501	4.0	3.9

Note: 000 omitted.

Figure 4. Worksheet for analysis of income statement

on future profits. Jones learns that cost of sales in 19X4 was 80 percent of sales, and he decides to find the cause of this unfavorable trend.

From other sources within the company he develops the following details of cost of sales and calculates their individual percentages of sales:

| | 19X6 | | 19X5 | | 19X4 | |
	Cost	% of Sales	Cost	% of Sales	Cost	% of Sales
Labor	$ 2,265	15.7%	$ 1,927	15.0%	$1,663	14.4%
Materials	5,870	40.7	4,983	38.9	4,183	36.2
Overhead	2,940	20.4	2,860	22.3	2,751	23.8
Other	700	4.9	670	5.2	650	5.6
Total	$11,775	81.7%	$10,440	81.4%	$9,247	80.0%

The table shows that both labor and material costs are increasing relative to sales. Jones consults with production engineering and manufacturing managers and finds that, except for occasional inefficiencies, labor standards are being met. Changes in product mix account for the increasing percentage in labor cost.

He then makes an analysis of material costs by product line and uncovers a problem in the industrial products line. The problem occurs in certain custom-made products because quoted prices do not fully reflect the most recent material cost increases. Cost of materials lists which are used for pricing custom-made products are updated every three months. In view of the more frequent changes in costs, Jones recommends, and the purchasing and sales managers agree, that monthly updates will be more appropriate.

The table also shows that the percentages of "overhead" and "other" costs are declining. However, Jones studies the details but finds nothing unusual. He will, of course, make an in-depth study of all costs when time permits.

ANALYZING THE BALANCE SHEET

To see more easily the relationship between the capital available to Noxton and how it is being invested, Jones restates the information on the balance sheet as shown in Figure 5. He draws from the balance sheet those items necessary to determine the total capital available. Total capital includes "long-term debt," "common stock," "capital surplus" and "retained earnings."

To arrive at the amount of capital invested, he calculates working capital by subtracting "current liabilities" from "current assets," adds in the value of "fixed assets" less depreciation and nets "other assets" with the "deferred income tax" liability. He draws these figures for 19X6 and 19X5 from the balance sheet shown in Figure 2 and the other years from prior years' statements that are available to him.

Through this restatement and subsequent analysis, Jones is trying to determine whether the company has the right amount of working and fixed capital for efficient operations. If the company has too much capital invested for the level of business, the excess amount will not earn a high enough rate of return. As a result, the total rate of return on capital available will drop.

Too little capital invested, for instance too small plant capacity or too low inventories, causes inefficiencies and profitable opportunities to be lost. Customers may order from competitors who are able to supply the product more quickly.

Balance Sheet Items	Capital Structure	19X6	19X5	19X4	19X3	19X2
Long-term debt, 8% notes	Long-term notes	$2,500	$2,500	$2,500	$2,500	$2,500
Stockholders' equity						
Preferred stock, 5% cumulative, $100 par value each; authorized 10,000 shares; issued and outstanding, none	Preferred stock	—	—	—	—	—
	Total senior capital	2,500	2,500	2,500	2,500	2,500
Common stock, $1 par value each; authorized—1,000,000 shares; issued and outstanding— 700,000 shares	Common capital	5,480	5,255	5,104	4,992	4,767
Capital surplus						
Retained earnings						
	Total capital available	$7,980	$7,755	$7,604	$7,492	$7,267

Capital Invested

Balance Sheet Items	Capital Structure	19X6	19X5	19X4	19X3	19X2
Current assets minus current liabilities	Working capital	$4,412	$4,012	$3,754	$3,742	$3,617
Net property, plant & equipment	Fixed capital (net)	3,793	3,918	4,000	3,900	3,675
Other assets minus deferred income taxes	Other (net)	(225)	(175)	(150)	(150)	(25)
	Total capital invested	$7,980	$7,755	$7,604	$7,492	$7,267

Note: 000 omitted.

Figure 5. Worksheet for restating balance sheet capital information for analysis

SYMPTOMS OF CAPITAL SIZE

Too much capital often shows up in larger cash balances than needed for capital investment or debt retirements over a reasonable period of time. Excessive receivables with past-due accounts, sluggish inventory turnover with obsolete and deteriorating stocks, underutilized plant capacity, are also signs of too much capital.

Too little capital shows up in shortages of cash, difficulties in making payments, stock shortages, production bottlenecks, and delays in making deliveries. The rate of return on capital invested may also be an indicator of excessive or short capital. Low rates of return can indicate too much capital. High rates can signal too little capital.

The right amounts of working and fixed capital will vary depending on the company's own situation and the type of industry. Many manufacturers tend toward equal amounts of working capital and fixed capital. Service businesses, however, normally require very little fixed capital. From his worksheets shown in Figure 5, Jones can see that Noxton's working capital has been increasing steadily in recent years, is now greater than fixed capital, comprising more than 50 percent of total capital invested. While such a change in the relationship between working and fixed capital does not necessarily indicate a problem, he wants to determine the need for this larger investment in working capital and will analyze selected working capital items as described later in this Section.

WHAT ANALYSIS OF FIXED CAPITAL SHOWS

With regard to the fixed capital, Jones knows that the plant is only seven years old and the average life of the machinery is about four years. He is told that the plant is now operating at about 75 percent of rated capacity. This will allow for anticipated growth over the next five years. Because plant construction costs have risen over recent years, Noxton may show a somewhat higher investment in fixed capital relative to working capital than competitors with older plants. However, Jones has no reason to believe there is excessive investment in fixed capital. In fact, he has been told by the production manager that additional presses and vacuum forming equipment are needed but that capital to buy them has not been made available for the past two years.

Figure 5 also shows the source of Noxton's capital. In his restatement of capital, Jones excludes the short-term bank notes that appear on the balance sheet from the capital available since they represent temporary funds for seasonal needs. He compares the long-term debt (8% notes) of $2,500,000 to total capital available and sees that it represents less than one-third of the total capital available. This is a conservative capital structure. Its effect on the common investors will be analyzed later.

If there were preferred stock outstanding, Jones would include it under senior capital. The balance sheet in Figure 2 classifies preferred stock under shareholders' equity. Preferred stock is neither debt nor equity, but it is senior to common. If either preferred stock or debt were convertible into common and there was a reasonable expectation that conversion would occur, Jones would have included it with the common capital in his restatement of capital in Figure 5.

Noxton does not have any long-term capital leases. Property financed with a long-term lease that does not appear on the financial statement would be included in senior capital and fixed capital when restating the capital accounts. Capital leases and other sources of capital are discussed later.

OTHER JUDGMENTS THAT CAN BE MADE FROM BALANCE SHEET ANALYSIS

Rapid increases in receivables or inventories may signal a loss in control and possibly be a warning of future write-downs. In the absence of explanatory information, quantitative information can be used for qualitative judgments and to spur the analyst to dig deeper.

The financial manager can make certain judgments regarding the fixed capital just from the balance sheet data. For instance, Noxton's depreciable assets (excludes land) totaled $4,900,000 at the end of 19X6. If 90 percent of this amount on average will be depreciated (10 percent residual value), then the depreciation in 19X6 of $325,000 (shown in Figure 3 "Statement of Changes in Financial Condition") indicates an average life of 13.5 years ($4,410,000 ÷ $325,000). The weighted average of plant and machinery and equipment would indicate a life of about 25 years for the plant and eight years average for the machinery and equipment. (Useful lives are usually given in the annual report.)

Dividing the accumulated depreciation of $1,557,000 (shown on the balance sheet in Figure 2) by the depreciable value of $4,410,000 shows that the assets on average are about 35 percent depreciated. Taken as a group, therefore, the assets are slightly less than six years old (13.5 years × .35). While this is not an indication of efficiency, Jones can make a judgment that the assets are relatively new and there is no urgent need to replace them in the near future.

ANALYZING THE STATEMENT OF CHANGES IN FINANCIAL POSITION

This statement shows the interplay between the balance sheet and the income statement. It helps identify the source of capital and how it is being used.

The statement format that shows Noxton's figures for 19X6 and 19X5 has been prescribed by the accounting profession. However, for analytical and planning purposes, Jones uses the format shown in Figure 6 that allows him to analyze cash items whenever possible to show actual cash flows.

For instance, the increase in deferred income tax liability, a non-cash item, is not shown. Instead, he uses the actual tax amounts paid. Thus the format enables Jones to concentrate on cash movements that affect cash balances and show financing requirements.

Jones starts to prepare the cash flow statement with the net profit *before* taxes as it appears on the Statement of Income (Figure 3). He adds back the depreciation which he finds on the Statement of Changes in Financial Condition (also part of Figure 3), giving total "sources of cash" of $1,425,000.

He then totals the cash used: capital expenditures appear as "additions to property, plant and equipment" on the Statement of Changes in Financial Condition, as do "dividends paid." He obtains the actual

	19X6	19X5
Source of cash		
Net profit before taxes	$1,100	$ 976
Depreciation	325	300
	1,425	1,276
Uses of cash		
Capital expenditures	200	250
Increase in current accounts	540	336
Taxes paid	445	395
Dividends paid	350	350
	1,535	1,331
Cash long/(short)	(110)	(55)
Financing		
New financing (short-term notes)	100	—
Cash (increase)/decrease	10	55

Note: 000 omitted.

Figure 6. Cash flow statement

amount of taxes paid in 19X6 of $445,000 from the treasurer of the company.

Jones calculates the increase in "current accounts" of $540,000 as shown in the following tabulation:

Current Accounts	*19X6*	*19X5*	*19X6 Change*
Accounts receivable	$1,472	$1,220	$ 252
Inventories	4,300	3,792	508
	5,772	5,012	760
Accounts payable	(1,160)	(980)	(180)
Other expenses payable	(430)	(390)	(40)
Total	$4,182	$3,642	$ 540

Note: 000 omitted.

The figures for the accounts listed are derived from the balance sheet shown in Figure 2. The "change" figure in the table shows the differences between these balance sheet figures. The differences, or changes, also show up on the "Statement of Changes in Financial Condition." The current accounts include receivables plus inventories and other current assets less accounts and other current payables. Taxes, dividends, and loans payable are excluded. The statement can be expanded, of course, to list each account separately. If any long-term loans had been retired during the year (in Noxton's case, none were), they would be included in the "financing" section.

A review of the cash flow statement (Figure 6) shows that the increase in current accounts of $540,000 in 19X6 was largely responsible for the cash shortage of $110,000 in that year. Jones notes from his tabulation the major cause of the increase in current accounts is the $508,000 growth of inventory. Because other uses of cash in 19X6 for capital expenditures, taxes, and dividends appear normal, he concludes that Noxton's ability to pay future dividends at either the current or a higher amount may well depend upon controlling the growth in inventory. He intends to bring this matter to the attention of top management.

Capital expenditures and increases in current accounts are "future oriented" in addition to being an historical record. Both commit capital for the purpose of producing future profits.

However, there must be good reasons for such commitments of capital or they will cause losses rather than profits. Jones must be aware of current events affecting the company. For example, a large increase in orders that caused an increase in production and inventory would probably ease his concern about the large commitment of capital. Therefore, he must examine the causes to be able to advise top management.

CALCULATING FREE CASH FLOW FOR PURPOSES OF ANALYSIS

Free cash flow is the cash available to investors from operations assuming that there is no long-term debt interest expense. Jones uses free cash flow as a rough measure of what investors might expect. He calculates it in the following table:

FREE CASH FLOW
(000 omitted)

	19X6	19X5
Dividends paid	$ 350	$ 350
Cash increase/(decrease)	(10)	(55)
Financing decrease/(increase)	(100)	—
Interest expense net of tax savings	105	103
Total	$ 345	$ 398

Cash available to investors includes the dividends that have been paid to them, in this case $350,000. However, as Jones' "Cash flow statement" (Figure 6) shows, the company is cash short by $110,000. In the free cash flow statement, therefore, he has shown this shortage by the "financing increase" of $100,000 and "cash decrease" of $10,000. Free cash flow analysis assumes, as mentioned before, no long-term debt interest expense, so Jones adds back this interest expense net of tax savings of $105,000 to arrive at a total free cash flow of $345,000 in 19X6.

What is important to the financial manager, to top management and to investors is not the amount but the direction of change from year to year. If free cash flow is positive over time, that fact may indicate that there are relatively few new investment opportunities for the company and that payment of relatively high dividends is appropriate.

If free cash flow is negative or declining, investors may lower their expectations of future profitability which may cause them to place a lower value on the company's stock. Or, they may expect that the additional investment of capital, which in Noxton's case has caused the recent declines in free cash flow, to provide a satisfactory rate of return in the months to come.

Jones knows he must focus on the additional investments being made in working capital, inventories and receivables for example, to assess their contribution to future profitability. This will be discussed in a later Section.

CASH ANALYSIS

Jones notes from the cash flow statement that cash has decreased for two consecutive years. As the financial manager he knows that another measure of the company's strength is the number of days operating expenses that can be covered should all cash receipts be suspended and whether that number of days has been increasing or declining. Jones uses the worksheet shown in Figure 7 to make this determination for the years 19X6 and 19X5.

Cash balances during the year may be quite different from the year-end position. But the calculation in Figure 7 shows a significant decrease in the company's ability to cover expenses. Through discussions with other managers, Jones learns that cash is tighter, and it is becoming

	19X6	19X5	19X6	19X5
Operating expenses (from Statement of Income)				
Cost of sales	$11,775	$10,440		
Selling and shipping expenses	725	670		
Administrative and general expenses	600	530		
	13,100	11,640		
Less: depreciation (from Statement of Changes in Financial Condition)	325	300		
Total cash operating expenses	$12,775	$11,340	$12,775	$11,340
Expenses per day (divide total operating expenses by 365 days)			35	31
Cash on hand including certificates of deposit (from Balance Sheet)			890	900
Number of days coverage (divide cash on hand by expenses per day)			25	29
Cash on hand (890 and 900) less current notes payable (600 and 500) from Balance Sheet			290	400
Number of days coverage without notes (divide cash on hand less current notes payable by expenses per day)			8	13

Note: 000 omitted.

Figure 7. Worksheet to determine number of days cash coverage of operating expenses

more difficult to meet supplier payment dates and to maintain the current levels of CDs.

Jones also learns that $300,000 of short-term notes must be repaid to the bank over the next three months. He plans to discuss this loss of liquidity with top management and make suggestions on how to improve the cash position. Noxton's short-term cash forecast shows a balance of only $100,000 six months from now after repayment of all short-term notes.

ANALYZING THE ACCOUNTS RECEIVABLE

Noxton's sales are almost entirely on credit. Jones decides to determine if a slowdown in turnover of receivables might be contributing to the cash shortage. He does so with the worksheet shown in Figure 8. While average days outstanding have increased from 35 in 19X5 to 37 in 19X6, the change is not large. Furthermore, the average is good according to the credit terms usually granted. Jones confirms with the credit manager that collections are running within current terms except for one or two customers who are consistently a few days late. After reviewing the aging analysis of accounts receivable and seeing no problem, Jones concludes that Noxton's investment in the receivables is reasonable, and not a primary cause of the declining liquidity.

	19X6	19X5
Sales (from Statement of Income, Figure 3)	$14,415,000	$12,836,000
Average daily sales (sales divided by 365 days)	39,493	35,167
Accounts receivable (from Balance Sheet, Figure 2)	1,472,000	1,220,000
Average days receivables outstanding (accounts receivable divided by average daily sales)	37	35

Figure 8. Testing turnover of accounts receivable

INVENTORY ANALYSIS

Jones knows that inventory has been increasing to meet the higher sales targets for the next year. He also knows that it is company policy to deliver products promptly and to meet scheduled delivery dates. He decides to check the turnover of inventory, and to learn what the trend of turnover has been over a period of time. The formula for calculating inventory turnover is:

cost of sales ÷ closing inventory = turnover rate

Taking the cost of sales from the income statement (Figure 3) and the closing inventory from the balance sheet (Figure 2) for 19X6 and 19X5, Jones finds:

Year	Cost of Sales		Closing Inventory		Turnover Rate
19X6	$11,775,000	÷	$4,300,000	=	2.74
19X5	$10,440,000	÷	$3,792,000	=	2.75

Checking further with previous years, he finds the turnover rate even lower. He concludes that the problem is not in a deteriorating turnover rate, but he is still concerned about the amount invested in inventories.

Because product lines are somewhat different and volume of sales has an effect, a comparison of inventory turnover with that of competitors may not produce an entirely reliable measure. However, Jones decides to compare Noxton's inventory turnover to that of several competitors. His calculations show that their turnovers range from 2.60 to 4.00.

One competitor with sales and product lines similar to Noxton's shows a turnover of 3.75. This indicates to Jones that Noxton might be able to operate with about a $1,100,00 lower inventory. He arrives at this conclusion by making the following calculations:

Cost of Sales		Turnover Rate		Closing Inventory
$11,775,000	÷	2.74	=	$4,300,000 (actual for 19X6)
$11,775,000	÷	3.75	=	$3,143,000 (projected at _____ competitor's rate)
				$1,157,000 potential _____ reduction

Also, finished goods on hand at Noxton are about 10 days higher than the competitor's, which represents about $300,000 invested.

Jones concludes that Noxton's inventory is too high notwithstanding the company's policy regarding meeting delivery schedules. Even a reasonable reduction in the level of inventory relative to sales would have a significant effect on the company's cash position. Jones decides to discuss this situation with the president and to get studies underway on purchasing policies, reorder levels, economic order quantities, finished stock levels, and labor hours. He will also look into disposing of excess stocks of raw materials and scrapping obsolete material.

Jones has now completed the first stage of analysis of Noxton's financial statements. He has detected an approaching liquidity problem unless steps are taken to prevent it. He believes that investment in assets is satisfactory except for inventory, and he has initiated actions and made recommendations that should result in improvement.

He is also alert to areas that could be of concern to investors. These include the recent reductions in operating margins, the loss of cash, and perhaps concern over excessive inventories which could result in future write-offs and lower profits. His actions are also directed to areas of concern to investors. This is important since investors, and lenders, are needed sources of additional capital.

III

Ratio Analysis: A Planning Tool

Ratio analysis helps managers, lenders, vendors, other creditors and investors determine trends in operating efficiency, rates of return on capital, credit worthiness, and the relationships between capital available and how it is being invested. Managers also use ratios as a planning tool. For instance, ratio analysis enables the financial manager to identify unfavorable relationships or trends and to advise management on possible corrective actions.

Ratios are computed from information in the financial statements. They show quantitative rather than qualitative data. Therefore, some care must be taken when interpreting them. For instance, a working capital ratio of 2:1 may seem weaker than one of 4:1. But if the 4:1 ratio reflects overdue receivables, obsolete inventory, and other current assets of doubtful value, then it may actually be weaker than the 2:1 ratio. *Quality* does count.

When interpreting ratios, management must consider that changes in one year may have little or no significance; each company differs in its operations and capital structure; industries differ; and values change periodically depending on economic and other factors. Also, in ratio analysis, the basic accounting information used to calculate the ratios must be consistent.

Despite these difficulties, ratios focus attention on key areas. Comparisons of results to other companies are easier because the information is given in percentage form. Industry standards for many ratios have evolved over the years. When a company does not meet these standards, its managers must seek valid causes and take corrective action when needed. Of course, standards can change as companies adopt new ones to meet current conditions. But each company must adopt only what is appropriate for itself.

SETTING GUIDELINES FOR RATIOS

Top executives, with the assistance of the financial manager, should review ratios periodically. They should know how their performance and policies affect them and what the implications are.

Jones, Noxton's new director of finance, wants to establish company guidelines for key ratios and then use these guidelines for operations and financial planning. The guidelines he develops will apply to Noxton only. But others can use his process of developing them and tailor guidelines to their own companies.

PROFIT RATIOS

The profit ratios include:

- sales to total capital
- adjusted net income to sales
- adjusted net income to total capital
- sales to common capital
- net income to sales
- net income to common capital.

These are the most important indicators of how effectively management is using available capital.

The relation between sales, from which profit is derived, and the total capital of the company is of particular interest because it helps the financial manager learn the productivity of the business in normal operations.

The ratio of sales to common capital gives some indication of how well the company is doing with the capital that the owners of the business have invested. Long-term borrowings are eliminated when calculating this ratio. However, a high ratio of sales to common capital does not necessarily mean that the company is doing well. It may simply mean that the company is too dependent on borrowed capital, an unhealthy fact. But if debt is not excessive, a high ratio shows that management has been successful in generating high sales with a small investment.

The other profit ratios, sometimes called earnings ratios, compare income (either adjusted or net) to sales, total capital, and common capital. The income to sales ratio, particularly year-to-year changes, give some clues to how earnings react to changes in sales. The trends show, to some degree, how well management is able to adjust costs to changes in sales, though earnings fluctuations will vary from industry to industry as well as from company to company.

The income to capital ratios show what the returns on the total and common investments are. These can be valuable to management in comparing results with those of other companies and to owners to determine whether they should consider alternative investments.

To begin the task of profit ratio analysis, Jones makes up the worksheet shown in Figure 9. He obtains the figure on line 2 from the balance sheet by adding long-term debt to common capital. He gets the amounts on lines 1, 4 and 7 from the statement of income. To determine the book income tax rate (line 8), Jones takes the provision for taxes from the statement of income and divides it by income before income taxes.

He fills in the figures for 19X6 on the worksheet and calculates the ratios. After he has included the prior years' figures on the worksheet, he will be able to see trends and changes from year to year.

CALCULATING THE RATIOS

To compute the ratios, Jones uses the capital outstanding at the *beginning* of the year. But the average or end of year capital can be used as well.

Line	Description	19X6	19X5	19X4	19X3	19X2	19X1
1	Net sales	$14,415					
2	Total capital beginning of year	$7,755					
3	Sales to total capital ratio (1 ÷ 2)	1.86					
4	Reported net income	$ 575					
5	Adjusted for extraordinary gains/losses	—					
6	Adjusted reported net income (4 ± 5)	$ 575					
7	Interest expense on long-term debt	$ 200					
8	Book income tax rate	.477					
9	1.000 minus book income tax rate	.523					
10	Interest expense net of taxes (7 × 9)	$ 105					
11	Adjusted net income (6 + 10)	$ 680					
12	Adjusted net income to sales ratio (11 ÷ 1)	.047					
13	Adjusted net income to total capital ratio (11 ÷ 2)	.088					
14	Common capital beginning of year	$5,255					
15	Sales to common capital ratio (1 ÷ 14)	2.74					
16	Net income to sales ratio (6 ÷ 1)	.040					
17	Net income to common capital ratio (6 ÷ 14)	.109					

Note: 000 omitted on $ figures.

Figure 9. Worksheet for profit ratios

Whatever approach the financial manager uses, he should use it consistently.

Jones also adjusts reported net income when comparing it to total capital (long-term debt plus common capital) by adding back interest expense net of income tax. The effect of this adjustment is to show for purposes of analysis the net income that would result if the common stockholders provided all the capital. This lets him develop the rates of return on an unleveraged (assuming the long-term debt is stockholders' capital) and leveraged basis (with long-term debt). The computation of adjusted net income to capital appears below:

UNLEVERAGED

		19X6	19X5
Net income as reported	(A)	$ 575	$ 501
Interest expense on long-term debt		200	200
Times 1.000 minus book income tax rate	(B)	105	103
Adjusted net income	(A) + (B)	680	604
Capital at beginning of year			
(includes long-term debt)	(C)	$7,755	$7,604
Adjusted net income to total capital	(B) ÷ (C)	.0876	.0794

No such adjustment to net income is made when comparing it to common stockholders' capital, however, since they absorb the interest cost after tax. This computation follows:

LEVERAGED

	19X6	19X5
Net income as reported	$ 575	$ 501
Common capital at beginning of year	5,255	5,104
Net income to common capital	.1094	.0982

ANALYZING THE PROFIT RATIOS

Jones computes the profit ratios for a five-year period and obtains the following results:

PROFIT RATIOS

Line		19X6	19X5	19X4	19X3	19X2
1	Sales to total capital	$1.860	$1.690	$1.650	$1.510	$1.420
2	Adjusted net income to sales	.047	.047	.047	.043	.048
3	Adjusted net income to total capital	.088	.079	.078	.065	.068
4	Sales to common capital	2.740	2.510	2.310	2.300	2.340
5	Net income to sales	.040	.039	.040	.034	.037
6	Net income to common capital	.109	.098	.092	.078	.087

Line 1 shows the amount of sales for each $1.00 of capital. While sales are increasing relative to the capital invested, the adjusted net income to sales (line 2) has remained constant for the past three years. However, Jones recalls that the *operating* quality of income in 19X6 was not quite equal to 19X5 because 19X6 had lower nonoperating expenses and a lower book income tax rate. This was also true for 19X5 compared to 19X4.

While ratios do not show quality, the financial manager can make judgments by adding pieces of information together. Line 3 shows the rate of return on total capital. It can be computed separately as was done on page 29 or by multiplying line 1 by line 2. Line 6 shows the return on common capital and the effect of leverage from long-term debt. From year to year this rate of return changes more radically than the rate of return on total capital (line 3).

It's clear that Noxton's rates of return on capital are highly dependent on the level of sales. This situation offers both opportunities and vulnerabilities. If sales do increase in 19X7, Noxton may do quite well. If sales do not increase, the results may be very disappointing. If Noxton can improve its adjusted net income to sales ratio (line 2), it will be less vulnerable to poorer than expected sales in the future.

Jones has already advised that material cost sheets be given more frequently to the sales department for pricing purposes. More rapid price adjustments will help in this area. The studies of inventory control also recommended may help to reduce costs, increase income and improve the adjusted net income to sales ratio.

How appropriate are Noxton's rates of return on capital? This question will be examined in the next Section. But Noxton's competitors in 19X6, Jones finds out, averaged a return on total capital of about 9.2

percent and on common about 11.5 percent. Therefore, Noxton is below average. It appears that there is some room for improvement.

In order to get a visual comparison of Noxton's sales to total capital ratio and adjusted net income to sales ratio to some of its competitors, Jones prepares the chart shown in Figure 10. On the right side of the chart he plots rates of "return on total capital" ranging from 6 to 14 percent. He then draws curves showing the various relationships between the two ratios—sales to total capital and adjusted net income to sales—that are necessary to achieve these rates of returns.

He then plots Noxton's two ratios on the chart and those of its major competitor, Excello Co. He also plots (indicated by x's) the ratios of six other competitors.

The chart illustrates the relationships between capital efficiency (sales to total capital) and operating efficiency (adjusted net income to sales) for selected rates of return on total capital. The lower the adjusted net income to sales, the higher must be the sales to total capital to obtain a given rate of return on total capital.

As the chart shows, four competitors have a better ratio than Noxton on adjusted net income to sales. Five have a better sales to total capital ratio. The Excello Company has product lines closest to Noxton's. It also has an estimated 11 percent share of the market. It appears that Noxton can realistically set goals to improve both ratios by lowering its cost of sales (and/or other cost reductions) and selling to get a higher share of the market. (Profit planning goals will be discussed in a later Section.)

EXAMINING THE EFFECT OF LEVERAGE

Jones next examines the effect of leverage on Noxton's common stockholders:

Source of Net Income	19X6 Amount	19X6 %	19X5 Amount	19X5 %
From operations	$461	8.8	$405	7.9
Tax saved on interest	95	1.8	98	1.9
Trading on common	19	0.4	(2)	—
Total income to common	$575	10.9 (rounded)	$501	9.8

Note: 000 omitted.

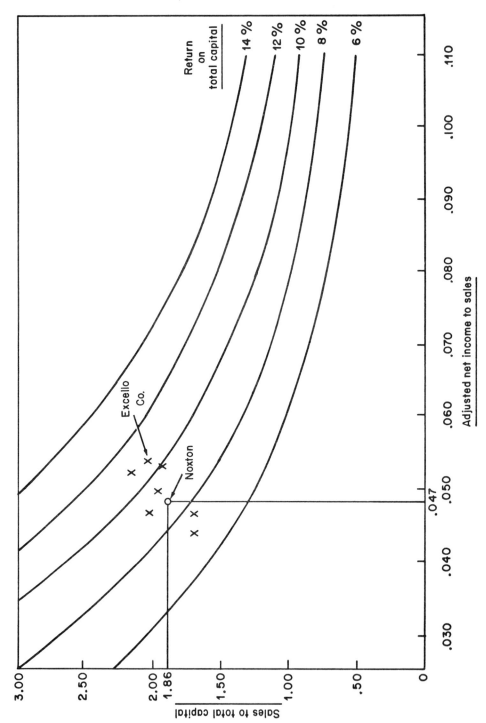

Figure 10. Relationships between capital efficiency and operating efficiency

To construct this table, Jones starts with the 8.8 percent adjusted net income to total capital for 19X6 (uses actual rate of .08768) shown on line 3 of the table on page 30 and applies it to the common capital at the beginning of the year of $5,255,000. The result, $461,000, is the income earned through operations only. The amount of the tax saved on interest expense is found by applying the book income tax rate of 44.7 percent to the $200,000 interest expense on long-term debt. The corresponding percentage is found by dividing the resultant $95,000 tax saved by $5,255,000. Trading on common is found by taking the difference between the operating rate of return (.08768) and the 8 percent interest rate on the long-term debt (.08) and applying it to the amount of long-term debt. The result is $19,000.

Jones sees that in 19X5, trading on common was negative because the 7.9 percent earned on total capital was below the 8.0 percent cost of the long-term debt. This was also true in prior years. What can be concluded? In 19X6 the common stockholders benefited for the first time from having earnings from operations provide a rate of return in excess of the cost of the long-term debt.

Of course, the common stockholders have benefited in past years from the tax savings on interest. But tax rates are largely beyond the control of the company's managers. In short, the leverage from debt from operating results only began to accrue to stockholders in 19X6. Also, if higher sales are realized in 19X7 at the 19X6 operating margins, the common stockholders will receive increased benefits. The estimates of these benefits can be made easily for various projected sales levels.

GROWTH RATIOS

Jones uses indices to make it easier to compute average growth per year and to determine relationship changes. He uses 19X1 as the base year and the worksheet shown in Figure 11. The amounts for lines 1, 3 and 5 appear on the statement of income. Total capital (line 7) and common capital (line 9) have already been determined on the worksheet for profit ratios (Figure 7).

Jones does his calculations for each year and arrives at the table shown on page 35:

Line	Description	Base Year 19X1	19X6	19X5	19X4	19X3	19X2
1	Net sales		$14,415				
2	Net sales divided by base	100.0	145.8				
3	Operating income		$ 1,315				
4	Operating income divided by base	100.0	147.8				
5	Net income		$ 575				
6	Net income divided by base	100.0	155.4				
7	Total capital		$7,980				
8	Total capital divided by base	100.0	104.8				
9	Common capital		$5,480				
10	Common capital divided by base	100.0	118.7				

Note: 000 omitted on $ figures.

Figure 11. Worksheet for growth ratios

GROWTH RATIOS
(19X1 + 100)

Line		% Average	19X6	19X5	19X4	19X3	19X2	19X1
7	Sales	7.8	145.8	129.8	116.8	111.0	109.2	100.0
8	Operating income	8.1	147.8	134.3	129.8	102.2	109.2	100.0
9	Net income	9.2	155.4	135.4	124.8	101.4	108.1	100.0
10	Total capital	0.9	104.8	101.8	99.8	98.4	94.7	100.0
11	Common capital	3.5	118.7	113.2	110.5	108.1	103.2	100.0

Sales and operating income have grown at nearly the same compound annual rate (7.8 and 8.1 percent, respectively) over the five-year period. But a lower growth trend in operating income can be seen by comparing lines 7 and 8 since 19X4. The average annual industry sales growth over this five-year period is about 8.5 percent and Jones calculates that Excello, Noxton's major competitor, has averaged about 8.9 percent.

While Noxton has held market share over the past three years, it has lost some ground over the past five. The 19X3 and 19X2 years include a recession period, so Jones is able to judge Noxton's vulnerability to a slow-down. Net income dropped about 6 percent in 19X3 against a slight increase in sales. Noxton also lost market share during these two years.

Lines 10 and 11 show a relatively low rate of capital growth. Jones attributes this slow growth to dividend payouts, which exceeded 60 percent of earnings; a low rate of earnings; and possibly a lack of investment opportunities. Jones knows that the capital budgets have been restricted during the past two years because of the company's cash position, not necessarily a lack of opportunities. If cash can be freed from the investment in inventory, it can make attractive capital investments in fixed assets. These should improve operating income, result in more capital inflow from operations and expand Noxton's total capital base.

The decrease in total capital (line 10) in 19X2 (from the base year 19X1 index of 100) reflects a long-term loan repayment in that year. The fact that some debt was retired and replaced does not change Jones' conclusion that Noxton would benefit from an expanded total capital base.

OPERATING RATIOS

The operating ratios include the relationship between sales and the major uses of capital: working capital, receivables, inventory, and net fixed assets.

Jones draws up another worksheet illustrated in Figure 12. Again, he obtains the figures on lines 1, 2, 3, 6, 8, 10, 12 and 14 from the statement of income and balance sheet. After making the calculations shown on the worksheet for each year, Jones assembles the operating ratios in the following table:

OPERATING RATIOS

Line		19X6	19X5	19X4	19X3	19X2
12	Sales to working capital	3.27	3.20	3.07	3.39	2.99
13	Sales to receivables	9.79	10.52	10.29	8.57	9.23
14	Sales to inventory	3.35	3.39	3.30	3.00	3.20
15	Cost of sales to inventory	2.74	2.75	2.60	2.40	2.57
16	Operating income to sales	.091	.093	.100	.083	.090
17	Sales to net fixed assets	3.80	3.28	3.00	2.93	2.96

Line 12 shows the sales to working capital ratio improving over the past two years. This ratio, a valuable adjunct to the sales to total capital ratio, is highly dependent on the level of sales, credit terms and payment records of customers, policy on deliveries, materials purchasing, and the time and labor required to convert raw materials into finished goods.

While Jones has already analyzed the turnover of receivables, as shown in Figure 8, and found them generally satisfactory, he uses a second method of analysis by relating sales directly to receivables. He divides sales by receivables and for 19X6 obtains a ratio of 9.79. This means that there were $9.79 in sales for every dollar of receivables. To change the ratio to a per-day basis, it need only be divided into 365 days:

$$\frac{\text{Days}}{\text{Ratio}} \quad \frac{365}{9.79} = 37 \text{ days}$$

Line	Description	19X6	19X5	19X4	19X3	19X2	19X1
1	Net sales	$14,445					
2	Current assets	$6,702					
3	Current liabilities	$2,290					
4	Working capital (2 − 3)	$4,412					
5	Sales to working capital ratio (1 ÷ 4)	3.27					
6	Accounts receivable	$1,472					
7	Sales to accounts receivable ratio (1 ÷ 6)	9.79					
8	Inventory	$4,300					
9	Sales to inventory ratio (1 ÷ 8)	3.35					
10	Cost of sales	$11,775					
11	Cost of sales to inventory ratio (10 ÷ 8)	2.74					
12	Operating income	$1,315					
13	Operating income to sales ratio (12 ÷ 1)	.091					
14	Net fixed assets	$3,793					
15	Sales to net fixed assets ratio (1 ÷ 14)	3.80					

Note: 000 omitted on $ figures.

Figure 12. Worksheet for operating ratios

The sales to receivables method is open to several qualifications. Most of Noxton's sales are made on credit. However, some companies make a large number of sales for cash. The sales total, therefore, contains a certain amount which has no relationship to receivables. If cash sales can be eliminated from total sales before the ratio is calculated, then this problem can be overcome.

Another qualification is that the sales figure represents the entire year. The receivables, however, are usually the result of transactions in the several weeks preceding the date of the balance sheet. If the business is of a seasonal nature, the preceding weeks may be either a low point or a high point in sales operations. Consequently, the receivables at the balance sheet date may not be the average of outstanding accounts for the entire sales year.

Another qualification on the accuracy and value of this ratio results from the effect of price changes, particularly sharp increases or decreases.

From the standpoint of investment in receivables, the most satisfactory condition exists when sales show a rising trend with increasing receivables ratios. Noxton's record over five years shows fluctuating ratios. The 19X6 ratio is lower than 19X5. This cannot be interpreted as a trend. But it does bear watching.

Jones has also analyzed the inventory (pages 23 and 24) and knows there can be some improvement on lines 14 and 15, sales to inventory and cost of sales to inventory. He believes that Noxton might be able to operate with about a $1 million reduction in inventory. But, considering the company's policy for prompt delivery, he believes that $500,000 might be a more reasonable target. If lines 14 and 15 were recomputed for 19X6 with a $500,000 lower inventory, the ratios would improve to 3.79 and 3.10, respectively.

COMPARISONS OF RATIOS

Jones knows that a ratio by itself gives little indication of whether the situation is good, average or poor. To determine its quality, a ratio should be compared with other ratios. He has compared Noxton's ratios for a series of years as shown in his worksheets and tables. However, comparison with those of other companies also provides valuable information.

The necessary information to calculate ratios for other companies is often not available, especially for privately owned, small and medium-sized companies. However, some trade associations and credit rating companies have compiled from their members or credit reports average or "standard" ratios for various industries. In such cases, the financial manager can compare the ratios for his company against industry averages to see deviations.

Jones does have the balance sheet and income statement for Noxton's major competition, Excello Company. His comparison of operating ratios follows:

	Noxton	Excello
Sales to working capital	3.27	3.96
Sales to receivables	9.79	8.69
Sales to inventory	3.35	4.68
Cost of sales to inventory	2.74	3.75
Operating income to sales	.091	.108
Sales to net fixed assets	3.80	4.21

He notes that Noxton is not as efficient as Excello in all areas except sales to receivables. Excello shows an average 42 days outstanding on receivables while Noxton is at 37. It occurs to Jones that Excello is in a better financial position to offer longer credit terms as a selling tool. In fact, if all competitors extended longer payment terms to customers, Noxton could lose sales and market share. Jones sees this as another reason to advise top management to reduce inventory to improve liquidity.

When Jones reviews sales to net fixed assets (line 17, page 36), the figures raise the question of how appropriate the ratio is. Noxton is currently operating at about 75 percent of capacity. If cost of sales in 19X6 at 75 percent capacity supports $14,415,000 in sales, 100 percent capacity would suggest sales should reach about $18,000,000. But Jones allows for items that don't affect capacity such as insurance and other overhead in cost of sales and estimates that about $20,000,000 in sales could be supported. This would mean a ratio of sales to net fixed assets of 5.25 to 5.50 before more plant capacity would be needed.

He asks about Excello's plant and learns that it is about 10 years older than Noxton's. Since construction costs would have been lower when Excello's plant was built and it has higher sales than Noxton, Jones concludes that the difference in ratios between the two companies is not significant. If Noxton had a 1 percent increase in market share (to 9 percent vs. Excello's 11 percent), Noxton's ratio would be 4.28, slightly higher than Excello's.

CREDIT RATIOS

These ratios (sometimes called working capital ratios) are used to appraise the immediate solvency of the company. Investors, whether lenders, trade creditors or providers of equity, are interested in the quality of the underlying assets. But immediate solvency plays a role too. For instance, long-term lenders are not willing to finance 100 percent of a company's assets no matter how high their quality because the rate of return would be too low for the risk. The common stockholders must assume a large share of this risk through their investment before lenders are willing to lend.

Rules of thumb have developed over the years for many of these ratios. Jones examines them carefully. If Noxton is departing from these "standards," the investors could penalize the company by higher interest rates, restriction of credit lines, onerous conditions on new borrowings, and the like.

Short-term lenders are primarily interested in the ability of the company to meet current obligations. The medium to long-term lenders are more interested in the company's earning capability over time, its ability to cover interest expense, and the quality of assets. Stock investors are interested in the company's earning ability.

RATIOS OF INTEREST PRIMARILY TO
SHORT-TERM LENDERS

Jones draws up the worksheet illustrated in Figure 13 as an aid to calculating ratios. He again turns to the balance sheet, statement of income and previous worksheets and tables for the figures that he needs.

After making the calculations, he extracts the ratios and lists them in a table as shown on page 41:

CREDIT RATIOS

Line		19X6	19X5	19X4	19X3	19X2
18	Current (working capital) ratio	2.92	3.07	3.04	3.15	3.21
19	Quick ratio	1.05	1.11	1.14	1.05	1.15
20	Receivables to working capital	.333	.304	.299	.342	.323
21	Days receivables outstanding	37	35	34	40	37
22	Inventory to working capital	.975	.945	.932	.978	.933
23	Current liabilities to tangible common	.423	.375	.360	.349	.344
24	Long-term debt to total capital (debt/equity)	.313	.322	.329	.334	.344
25	Long-term debt interest covered	2.9	2.5	2.3	2.0	2.0
26	Total liabilities to tangible common	.940	.905	.850	.849	.869

On line 18 Jones sees that the current or working capital ratio is normally about 3:1. While the ratio exceeds a long accepted rule of thumb, 2:1, he does not see it as a sign of strength. He knows companies in the industry carry large inventories and also that Noxton has too much inventory. If Noxton's inventory could be reduced by $500,000, the quality of working capital would be improved.

Because inventory is the least liquid of the current assets, the quick ratio (line 19) was developed to show a company's ability to pay current obligations out of cash and receivables. Noxton's quick ratio is barely acceptable since 1:1 is the least that many short-term lenders and trade creditors will accept. A reduction of inventory by $500,000 would increase the ratio to 1.27:1, a more comfortable margin.

Jones has already reviewed receivables. Lines 20 and 21 confirm his analysis. He will be alert for any increase in longer credit terms extended to customers.

Inventory to working capital (line 22) exceeds a commonly accepted standard of .800. Inventory in excess of .800 usually causes difficulties in meeting current obligations. A reduction in inventory by $500,000 would improve the ratio to about .800. Jones would prefer an inventory reduction of more than $500,000, but believes such an amount to be a realistic, current target.

CURRENT AND LONG-TERM LIABILITIES TO CAPITAL

Current liabilities to tangible common capital (line 23) tells the short-term lenders (which include trade creditors) how much they have in-

Line	Description	19X6	19X5	19X4	19X3	19X2	19X1
1	Current assets	$6,702					
2	Current liabilities	$2,290					
3	Working capital (1 − 2)	$4,412					
4	Current (working capital) ratio (1 ÷ 2)	2.93					
5	Inventory	$4,300					
6	Quick assets (1 − 5)	$2,402					
7	Quick ratio (6 ÷ 2)	1.05					
8	Accounts receivable	$1,472					
9	Accounts receivable to working capital ratio (8 ÷ 3)	.333					
10	Net sales ÷ 365 days = daily orders (000 omitted)	39					
11	Days receivables outstanding (8 ÷ 10) (in days)	37					
12	Inventory to working capital ratio (5 ÷ 3)	.975					
13	Common capital less intangibles	$5,415					
14	Current liabilities to tangible common ratio (2 ÷ 13)	.423					
15	Long term debt	$2,500					
16	Total capital (debt + equity)	$7,980					
17	Long term debt to total capital ratio (15 ÷ 16)	.313					
18	Long term debt interest expense	$ 200					
19	Net Income	$ 575					
20	Long term debt interest covered (19 ÷ 18)	2.9					
21	Total liabilities	$5,090					
22	Total liabilities to tangible common ratio (21 ÷ 13)	.940					

Note: 000 omitted on $ figures.

Figure 12. Worksheet for credit ratios—short-term interests

vested for each dollar invested by the company's owners in tangible assets. This ratio is affected by the long-term debt in a company's capital structure.

Noxton has a ratio of long-term debt to total capital (line 24) of about 31 percent. If a working capital ratio of about 3:1 is adequate (Jones believes it is), then the current liabilities to tangible common ratio on line 23 is reasonable. If Noxton had a less conservative long-term debt to total capital of 50 percent, the short-term lenders would be investing $.555 for each $1.00 of common.

He next calculates the ratio assuming the short-term bank notes are paid off and finds it is .313. Jones now has a range for this ratio of .313 to .555, and the .423 in 19X6 is about the middle. Any increase might be considered as risky. Creditors and short-term lenders prefer current liabilities to tangible common to be low because they regard the ownership as buffers protecting them from loss.

Line 24 shows long-term debt to total capital. It focuses attention on the extent to which the company depends on long-term borrowing for its funds. Line 25 shows how many times interest on the long-term debt is covered by net income. Interest is covered 2.9 times in 19X6. Normally 2.0 times is an acceptable minimum and Noxton did not fall below 2.0 even in 19X3, a recession year. The interest coverage is of particular concern to present and potential long-term lenders who want to be sure that earnings will safely cover interest payments.

Line 26, total liabilities to tangible common, shows an increasing trend approaching a usually accepted limit of 1.00. Since Noxton is using its maximum bank credit line, Jones feels that *additional* credit would be difficult and expensive to arrange. Excluding the short-term notes, however, would make the ratio .830, and that is a reasonable amount for Noxton with its current capital structure.

CAPITAL RATIOS OF IMPORTANCE TO LONGER-TERM INVESTORS

Jones next looks at the ratios dealing with capital structure. He prepares a worksheet as shown in Figure 14. He then draws up the table on page 45:

Line	Description	19X6	19X5	19X4	19X3	19X2	19X1
1	Common capital	$5,480					
2	Total assets	$10,570					
3	Common capital to total assets ratio (1 ÷ 2)	.518					
4	Long-term assets (net)	$3,793					
5	Long-term debt	$2,500					
6	Long-term assets (property, plant and equipment) to long-term debt ratio (4 ÷ 5)	1.52					
7	Long-term assets to common capital ratio (4 ÷ 1)	.692					
8	Working capital	$4,412					
9	Working capital to long-term debt ratio (8 ÷ 5)	1.76					

Note: 000 omitted on $ figures.

Figure 14. Worksheet for capital ratios

CAPITAL RATIOS

Line		19X6	19X5	19X4	19X3	19X2
27	Common capital to net total assets	.518	.528	.540	.541	.535
28	Long-term assets to long-term debt	1.52	1.57	1.54	1.50	1.46
29	Long-term assets to common capital	.692	.746	.754	.751	.766
30	Working capital to long-term debt	1.76	1.60	1.50	1.50	1.45

Line 27 shows that the common stockholders are supporting a little more than 50 percent of the asset values. This ratio also depends on the capital structure. While Jones knows the long-term debt ratio is conservative, total liabilities to tangible common are approaching the usually accepted limit. If a reduction in inventory was used to pay off the short-term notes of $600,000, the ratio would improve to .550 and still leave a reasonable amount of cash available.

The ratios on lines 28 and 29 show the long-term assets (property, plant and equipment) in relation to long-term debt and common capital. The amount of long-term assets should be reasonable or balanced in terms of total assets required to run the business efficiently. Long-term assets in manufacturing companies normally range from 40 to 60 percent of total assets.

If the values of long-term assets (property, plant and equipment) are too high, showing a chronic condition of idle capacity, the company will have lower rates of return on capital than competitors who use their capital more efficiently. Very high ratios on lines 28 and 29, therefore, may be signs of problems. Very low ratios may indicate an old, inefficient plant or need for major capital investments.

For example, if long-term assets are 40 percent of total assets, with a current (working capital) ratio of 3:1 and a long-term·debt to equity ratio of 1:2, the ratios on lines 28 and 29 will be approximately 1.50 and .75, respectively. Jones believes from his analysis of the sales to net fixed assets ratio of 3.80 that Noxton has neither an excess or shortage of production capacity and that the ratios on lines 28 and 29 are reasonable. He notes, however, that the ratios have decreased in

19X6, reflecting a lower level of new capital expenditures. He believes this should not continue if Noxton is to maintain a well-equipped efficient plant.

Line 30 shows that long-term debt is well within acceptable guidelines. Ordinarily, long-term debt should not exceed working capital, a ratio of 1.00. Jones notes that while this ratio has improved since 19X4, it is not necessarily a sign of strength since some of the improvement reflects excess inventory. The ratio, itself, however, is acceptable.

RECOMMENDATIONS FOR IMPROVING FINANCIAL POSITION

Jones now reviews all the critical ratios to suggest goals which would result from an inventory reduction of $500,000. He does this by restating the 19X6 balance sheet to show lower inventory with repayment of the short-term notes.

	Actual	Goal	Action Required
Working capital (current ratio)	2.9	3.6	Reduce inventory—pay notes
Quick ratio	1.1	1.3	Reduce inventory—pay notes
Inventory to working capital	.98	.80	Reduce inventory
Current liabilities to common	.42	.35	Pay notes
Total liabilities to common	.94	.83	Pay notes
Common capital to total assets	.52	.55	Reduce inventory—pay notes

If Noxton can meet these goals, it will be stronger financially and better able to:

1. invest in new machinery to improve operating costs,
2. respond to possible competitive actions that give longer credit to customers,
3. present a stronger argument for an increase in credit lines.

Noxton will also be perceived by investors as a stronger, more flexible company.

SUMMARY OF FINDINGS FROM ANALYSIS

Noxton is growing and its financial results, while not outstanding, are respectable. The company is conservatively financed, has a relatively modern plant and capacity for some growth. It is investing in new machinery at less than a satisfactory rate due to recent cash limitations. There is no current need for additional permanent financing. Long-term debt repayments start in two years, and planning to replace that debt will start next year. Jones wants Noxton to be seen by lenders as a stronger company before discussions for debt replacement are held with them.

In summary, 19X6 was a relatively good year for profit and return on investment. But many others in the industry achieved better results. Cash is tight and inventories are too high for the level of sales. Jones has started actions to reduce inventory in relation to sales, increase operating margins, and improve the overall financial structure of the company. He is keeping top management informed of developing problems affecting the financial integrity of the company and actively participating in bringing about needed improvements.

IV

The Role and Calculation of Cost of Capital

Noxton's capital consists of long-term debt and common stock. The long-term debt notes are held by Statewide Insurance Company. The stock is distributed among approximately 1,100 stockholders. Noxton has short-term credit lines of $600,000 from two banks. But these funds cover seasonal working capital requirements. They are not long-term capital.

Supply and demand create a competitive market for capital much the same as for manufactured products. Capital also has a cost. For example, Statewide Insurance must cover its costs of operation and make a profit for the risk of particular investments it makes. In Noxton's case, the compensation to Statewide was fixed at 8 percent in 19X1 when the loan was arranged.

Common stockholders also have costs to consider. They have investment alternatives involving different degrees of risk. They expect higher rates of return on their investment than if they invested in less risky government securities or in corporate bonds.

A successful company must earn its cost of capital over a period of time if it is to attract new capital to grow. What amount of profit is needed to satisfy the company's investors? This question can be answered by determining a company's cost of capital.

Jones wants to calculate Noxton's cost of capital and see how the profit goals relate to it. Since he thinks that the company will benefit from additional investment in machinery and equipment, he also wants to establish acceptable rates of return on capital investments for management's guidance. He knows that use of cost of capital as a benchmark results in better decision making. It also provides a way to allocate the company's capital to the most profitable opportunities.

COST OF CAPITAL IS AN AVERAGE

Cost of capital reflects the judgments of investors about business in general, different industries, and specific companies. It therefore varies among companies due to differences in growth prospects, capital structure, cyclical factors, management quality, perceived risk and other factors. Cost of capital is constantly changing. This is shown by the daily changes in market prices of publicly traded securities.

However, managers must operate during good times and bad. Once profit goals are set, a considerable amount of effort is required to achieve them. Changing profit goals too often would lead to chaos. Therefore, profit goals must satisfy investors *over time*. It is therefore an estimate based on average market conditions over the foreseeable future. Although it is an estimate, cost of capital is a valuable, reliable measure.

THE COST OF SENIOR SECURITIES

Noxton has only one security senior to common, the 8 percent long-term notes. Noxton has authorized, but unissued, preferred stock. Jones will determine its cost purely for informational purposes.

Noxton does not have any securities convertible into common stock. If there were convertible bonds or preferred stocks, Jones would assign to them the same cost as common capital regardless of their interest rate or dividend so that profit goals would cover the higher number of common shares after conversion occurs. If for some reason conversion was not anticipated, however, he would give them the cost of comparable senior securities that are *not* convertible. Interest and dividends on convertibles are usually lower because of the convertible feature.

HOW TO CALCULATE THE COST OF LONG-TERM DEBT

The 8 percent notes were bought by Statewide Insurance in 19X1 in a private placement. Because negotiations were handled directly, there was no commission although there were legal and auditing fees.

Jones calculates the cost on the 8 percent notes and compares it to cost estimates of 8 percent bonds sold in public offerings. While it is unlikely that Noxton could have sold bonds publicly in 19X1 without a higher interest rate, Jones wants to see the effect underwriting commissions, printing costs, legal and auditing fees have on debt cost.

His analysis is shown in Figure 15. It shows that publicly sold bonds with a 20-year maturity will cost about 0.3 percent more than a private sale of 12-year notes (public issue effective cost 8.4 percent versus private issue effective cost of 8.1 percent.) He assumes that future long-term borrowing by Noxton will follow past practice with a private placement.

Jones must calculate what Noxton's cost of capital would be currently for long-term debt. He has talked informally with Statewide Insurance about interest rates and learns that it is currently lending to prime credit companies at about 8.75 percent. Since Noxton is not considered prime, its present rate might range from 9.25 to 9.50 percent. To estimate the average cost of long-term debt Jones prepares the worksheet shown in Figure 16. The worksheet (using some data compiled by an investment service) shows the yields to maturity on publicly issued industrial bonds.

On the worksheet Jones lists the yields to maturity on all new public issues of industrial bonds since 19X1 as well as the yields on outstanding industrial bonds. He also lists the yields on outstanding *medium grade* industrial bonds because Noxton's bonds would be in this category if they were issued to the public. Medium quality bonds are neither highly protected by the number of times interest is covered by

	Noxton's 8% Notes	Public Issue 8% Bonds at Par (100)	Public Issue 8¼% Bonds at 102½
Total liability	$2,500,000	$2,500,000	$2,500,000
Commissions (estimated)	—	150,000	150,000
Printing, legal, audit costs	25,000	50,000	50,000
Total costs	$ 25,000	$ 200,000	$ 200,000
Annual cost			
Interest cost	$ 200,000	$ 200,000	$ 206,250
Amortization of costs	2,083*	10,000†	10,000†
(Premium)/discount amortization	—	—	(3,125)‡
Total annual cost	$ 202,083	$ 210,000	$ 213,125
Effective cost = total annual cost ÷ total liability	.081	.084	.085¶

*Costs of $25,000 are amortized over 12 years.
†Costs of $200,000 are amortized over 20 years.
‡Bonds sold at 102½ for a premium of $62,500. The premium is amortized over 20 years.
¶Bond yield tables give a slightly lower cost.

Figure 15. Analysis of effective interest cost

earnings nor are they poorly secured by asset values. Therefore, they have higher yields, at higher cost to the company, than do higher grade bonds.

The cost of long-term debt is related to new issue bond yields. New bond issues must often be sold at higher yields than comparable issues outstanding because of the added supply of bonds. On the worksheet Jones calculates that the average yield on new issues for the 19X1–19X6 period of 8.59 percent is about the same as on outstanding bonds of 8.60 percent. At times the bond market will put a premium on new issues. The demand for them means lower interest rates can be offered.

	All Grades Industrial New Issues	All Grades Industrial Outstanding	Noxton's Grade Medium Grade Industrial Outstanding
19X6	8.80%	8.80%	9.20%
19X5	8.28	8.30	8.90
19X4	8.61	8.84	9.67
19X3	9.12	9.25	10.26
19X2	8.87	8.78	9.14
19X1	7.86	7.60	8.07*
Total 19X1-X6	51.54%	51.57%	55.24%
Average 19X1-X6	8.59†	8.60%†	9.21%

Adjust to new issue basis (8.59% − 8.60%)   —

Adjust for financing costs (public offer .40%; private placement .10%)†   .40%

Average cost 19X1-X6 (public offer) =
9.21% + .40%†   =   9.61%

Average cost 19X1-X6 (private placement) =
9.21% + .10%†   =   9.31%

*Noxton borrowed at 8% from Statewide Insurance Company.
†See effective costs (Figure 15) for public offerings vs. private placement.

Figure 16. Yields on industrial bonds

At other times it is necessary to offer a higher yield. Comparing the yields in Figure 16 shows that this occurred in 19X2.

Jones has listed the yields on new issues and outstanding issues for all grades of industrial bonds because it is necessary to adjust outstanding bond yields to estimate new issue yields. For example, there are often not a sufficient number of new issues in medium grade industrial bonds to get a representative sample over a period of time.

Jones sees from his listing that the average spread between new issue and outstanding issue yields on all grades is not significant. So he does not have to adjust outstanding medium grade yields to convert them to a new issue basis. But it is necessary to adjust the yields for commissions (if any), printing, legal, and audit fees as shown in Figure 15.

Referring to his worksheet (Figure 16), Jones believes the average yield on outstanding medium grade industrial bonds of 9.21 percent for the period 19X1–19X6 is representative of Noxton's long-term debt cost in the foreseeable future. He adds .10 percent for estimated costs of legal and audit services (from Figure 15) and arrives at a total cost for private placement of long-term debt to Noxton of 9.31 percent.

The 9.31 percent interest cost suggests a precision that isn't exact because cost of capital is an estimate. Jones decides to round the estimate to 9.5 percent. Assuming a corporate income tax rate of 48 percent, the after-tax cost of long-term debt to Noxton becomes 4.94 percent (9.5% × [1.00 − .48] = 4.94).

CALCULATING THE COST OF PREFERRED STOCK

The cost of preferred stock is determined much the same as for long-term debt. Yields on various grades of preferred stock are published by Moody's Investors Services, Inc., which specializes in bond rating and compilations of security statistics. Jones believes Noxton's preferred stock would fall in the "speculative" category if it were issued. The average yield on speculative grade preferred stocks for the period 19X2-19X6 was approximately 8.5 percent. Since Noxton's preferred stock (par value $100) carries a dividend rate of only 5 percent, its average market value would be $58.82 to yield 8.5 percent ($100 × 5% ÷ 8.5% = $58.82). Financing and other costs in issuing preferred stock are usually higher than those for long-term bonds, so Jones adds .70 percent to 8.5 percent to arrive at a total cost of 9.2 percent for Noxton. Preferred stock dividends are not tax deductible. Therefore, 9.2 percent would also be Noxton's cost of preferred stock after tax.

HOW TO CALCULATE THE TRUE COSTS OF LEASES

Noxton has not leased any equipment. However, E.J. Carlson, president, has sent Jones a proposal from the RST Leasing Group. RST leases equipment to manufacturers. Its proposal says that leasing conserves working capital and provides low cost financing. Carlson wants an opinion from Jones on whether Noxton should lease some of the equipment needed by the manufacturing division. Jones must now calculate the costs of leasing compared to costs of financing equipment purchases by borrowing.

The two principal kinds of leases are operating and capital. Operating leases are not usually considered to be a means of permanent financing. Examples of operating leases include office space, short-term rental of special equipment for a specific project, rentals in order to obtain servicing or maintenance, and the like. The term of such leases is substantially less than the useful life of the equipment rented. These leases can be analyzed as operating costs.

Capital leases, however, are essentially substitutes for long-term debt. The equipment is leased for most of its useful life. The lease payments are, in effect, a combination of interest and principal payments. Capital leases, as is true for other sources of capital, have a cost. The RST proposal is a capital lease and Jones must determine its cost. If Noxton intends to lease equipment, its cost must be included in the cost of capital.

There is a practical limit on debt, including capital leases, as a percent of total capital. When debt gets too high, lenders charge higher interest rates and require onerous terms in loan agreements. Lenders make the same assumption as Jones does: capital leases should be considered as long-term debt.

Jones believes Noxton can safely carry long-term debt of about one-third of total capital. The ratio is now 31.3 percent, as he summarized in the table on page 41, line 24. He calculates that Noxton could add about $235,000 of capital leases *provided the cost is attractive and the funds are required.* He makes the following calculations:

DEBT TO TOTAL CAPITAL AFTER LEASES

Long-term debt	$2,500,000
Leases (add)	235,000
Total debt adjusted	$2,735,000

Capital available	$7,980,000
Leases (add)	235,000
Total capital adjusted	$8,215,000

$$\frac{\$2,735,000}{\$8,215,000} = 33.3\%$$

Jones also knows that the leased equipment must generate a profit or rate of return not just in excess of the lease cost but in excess of Noxton's weighted average cost of capital. A profit goal that simply equals debt or lease costs provides nothing for the common stockholders while exposing them to additional risk.

COMPARING COST OF LEASING AGAINST COST OF PURCHASING WITH DEBT

Before Jones can answer President Carlson's question about whether the company should lease equipment, he will have to compute Noxton's cost of common capital and obtain the weighted average cost of debt (including leases) and common. He will also review the requests for machinery and equipment to determine their contribution to profitability.

Jones first computes the cost of RST's lease proposal. For a five-year lease, RST is quoting $25.38 per $100.00 of principal value per year. The annual payment for five years of $25.38 is, in effect, an annual annuity that has a present value of $100.00

From annuity tables (available in texts on finance), Jones determines that the interest rate that discounts five annual payments of $25.38 to $100.00 is 8.5 percent. The partial annuity table that follows illustrates:

ANNUITY WHICH $1.00 WILL BUY

Periods n	6%	7%	8%	8.5%	9%
1	1.0600	1.0700	1.0800	1.0850	1.0900
2	.5454	.5531	.5608	.5646	.5685
3	.3741	.3811	.3880	.3915	.3951
4	.2886	.2952	.3019	.3053	.3087
5	.2374	.2439	.2505	.2538	.2571

Since the lease payment was quoted on an annual basis, five periods equals five years. As the table shows, and as appears in the box in the table, for five periods (years), $.2538 would be the annuity that $1 will buy at 8.5 percent. Or $100 will buy a $25.38 annuity for five years. To put it another way, 8.5 percent is the interest rate that discounts five annual payments of $25.38 to $100.00.

If the lease equipment will be completely worthless at the end of the five-year lease, 8.5 percent is the effective cost of the lease before tax. However, leased equipment normally has a useful life slightly in excess of the lease period. There is some residual value.

For example, if Noxton leases equipment and pays rent for it over five years but receives only 90 percent of its useful life, there is a 10 percent loss to Noxton in residual value. If this 10 percent ($10.00 for each $100.00) is added to the lease cost in year 5 when the lease terminates, the *effective lease cost* to Noxton increases to 10.9 percent before tax. The longer the lease term, the less effect the loss of residual value has on the rate because it must be discounted for more years. *But it is normally a significant factor in most capital leases.*

To obtain the 10.9 percent cost, it is necessary to use discounted cash flow techniques which are discussed in Section V. The tables, lease and loan amortization schedules in Figure 17 illustrate, however, how residual value does affect the rate.

If Noxton borrows $100.00 at 8.5 percent interest for five years and buys the equipment, the common stockholders will have an investment of $10.00 (the residual value) at the end of five years when the loan is paid off. This is shown in the loan amortization schedule at 8.5 percent in Figure 17. The equipment can either be sold, used or written off for tax purposes which will produce some savings in income taxes. These benefits are not available to Noxton if the equipment is leased.

Jones must now compute the after-tax cost of leasing. The after-tax cost of leasing compared to purchasing with borrowed capital is affected by the depreciation method used. Noxton uses for tax purposes the sum of the years digits method. (This is for illustration only. Allowable tax methods should be used.) Also, any loss in the investment tax credit by leasing must be included in the analysis to make a fair comparison between leasing and purchasing. Lease payments are tax deductible. But there are also tax deductions in the U.S. available to purchasers of equipment for the investment tax credit and depreciation.

LEASE AMORTIZATION SCHEDULE AT 10.9%

Assumption: Noxton leases equipment for five years on leasing company's terms.

Year	Lease Principal Beginning of Year	Annual Lease Payment	10.9% Interest on Principal	Reduction in Principal	Lease Principal End of Year
1	$100.00	$25.38	$10.90	$14.48	$85.52
2	85.52	25.38	9.32	16.06	69.46
3	69.46	25.38	7.57	17.81	51.65
4	51.65	25.38	5.63	19.75	31.90
5	31.90	25.38	3.48	21.90	10.00*

LOAN AMORTIZATION SCHEDULE AT 8.5%

Assumption: Noxton borrows at 8.5% for five years and purchases equipment.

Year	Loan Principal Beginning of Year	Annual Loan Payment	8.5% Interest on Principal	Reduction in Principal	Loan Principal End of Year	Depreciated Value†	Common Stock Investment
1	$100.00	$25.38	$ 8.50	$16.88	$83.12*	$82.00	$(1.12)‡
2	83.12	25.38	7.07	18.31	64.81	64.00	(.81)
3	64.81	25.38	5.51	19.87	44.94	46.00	1.06
4	44.94	25.38	3.83	21.55	23.39	28.00	4.61
5	23.39	25.38	1.99	23.39	—	10.00	10.00

*$10.00 represents loss of residual value to Noxton at lease termination date and additional income to RST Leasing which can sell the equipment or lease it again for a short period. RST has received $100.00 for the equipment plus 8.5% interest plus $10.00 for an effective rate of 10.9%.
†Based on straight line depreciation of 90% of equipment value for 5 years.
‡Common stock investment represents difference between loan principal outstanding at end of year and depreciated value.

Figure 17. Lease and loan amortization schedules

Year	Leasing		Purchasing				(2) + (6)		
	(1)	(2)	(3)	(4)	(5)	(6)	(7)		
	Lease Payment	Cost After 48% Tax	Sum of Years Digits Depreciation	Depreciation Tax Savings	Investment Tax Credit	Total Tax Savings	Lease Cost in Excess Purchasing	Present Value at 8%*	Present Value at 9%*
1	$ 25.38	$13.20	$33.33	$16.00	$6.67	$22.67	$ 35.87	$ 33.21	$32.90
2	25.38	13.20	24.00	11.52	—	11.52	24.72	21.19	20.81
3	25.38	13.20	18.00	8.64	—	8.64	21.84	17.34	16.86
4	25.38	13.20	12.00	5.76	—	5.76	18.96	13.94	13.43
5	25.38	13.20	2.67	1.28	—	1.28	14.48	16.66	15.91
Residual	—	10.00					10.00		
Total	$126.90	$76.00	$90.00	$43.20	$6.67	$49.87	$125.87	$102.34†	$99.91

*Use compound discount tables

†Present value of lease is $100.00. Interpolation to find effective cost is:

$$8\% + 1\% \times \frac{102.34 - 100.00}{102.34 - 99.91} = 8.67\%$$

Figure 18. After-tax cost of leasing compared to after-tax cost of purchasing

To compute the after-tax cost of leasing, therefore, it is necessary to determine the lease cost *after tax* in excess of the *tax savings* available to a purchaser. Jones prepares the schedule in Figure 18 showing the annual cash cost of leasing after taxes (column 7). By leasing, the company has an after-tax cost of $13.20, shown in column 2. But by leasing, it loses the tax savings that it would obtain by purchasing as shown in column 6. Therefore, the total lease cost in excess of purchasing is the sum of these two columns, in year 1 amounting to $35.87 and $125.87 for five years.

He discounts these annual cash costs at 8 and 9 percent and finds present values of $102.34 and $99.91, respectively. Since the present value (cost of equipment) is $100.00, he knows the *effective lease cost after tax* is between 8 and 9 percent, and through interpolation computes the cost at 8.67 percent. Therefore, leasing from RST will cost Noxton 8.67 percent after tax compared to long-term debt cost after tax of 4.94 percent.

Jones concludes that RST's quote is not as attractive as it first appears. Also, he is not sure that Noxton needs to lease equipment in order to release funds for other investment if inventory can be reduced as planned.

He decides to wait before making any recommendation to President Carlson until the capital budget information is reviewed. If additional capital that can be made available through leasing can be profitably invested at a rate greater than the weighted average cost of capital rate (long-term debt + leasing + common capital cost), he may then suggest that several leasing companies submit bids to be sure that Noxton gets the lowest possible lease cost.

THE COST OF COMMON CAPITAL

The common stockholder and the bondholder both look to *future results* to obtain a rate of return. The bondholder can compute his yield to maturity based on current market prices. The stockholder, however, must rely on future earnings, dividends, and appreciation in stock value and relate estimates to current market values. The following table illustrates:

	Bondholder 8.3% Interest Rate	Stockholder Company A		Stockholder Company B	
Current market value	$100.00	$100.00		$100.00	
Interest/earnings/ dividends expected per annum					
	Interest	Earnings	Dividends	Earnings	Dividends
Year 1	$8.30	$8.30	$4.15	$8.30	$ 0
Year 2	8.30	8.65	4.32	8.99	0
Year 3	8.30	9.00	4.50	9.73	0
Expected market value end of year 3	$100.00	$112.95		$127.02	
Expected rate of return	8.3% (Interest yield 8.3%)	8.3% (Dividend yield 4.15% + compound growth rate 4.15%)		8.3% (Dividend yield 0% + compound growth rate 8.3%)	

The table can be extended for any number of years. If bondholders or stockholders as a group decided that 8.3 percent was too low, the current market price of the securities would fall below $100.00. The table is illustrative of the principle only. In practice, it is not likely that stockholders would value Company A and Company B the same in view of the differences in dividend policy. And, too, stockholders would also want a higher rate of return than bondholders because of the greater risk.

To determine the cost of common capital, the financial manager must estimate what *investors* expect in earnings. It is also necessary to adjust the market price for financing and other costs of a new stock issue. Increasing the supply of stock will create pressure on its price. Existing stockholders are sometimes given rights to subscribe to the new shares at a lower price. As a result, the company receives less than market value with a new issue. The amounts will differ depending on market conditions, the size and quality of the issue, commissions, printing, legal, audit, and other costs. As a rule of thumb, a 10 to 20 percent reduction in the amount received can be expected: 10 percent less for major, well-regarded companies; 15 percent for middle-sized companies; and 20 percent for smaller, less-known companies.

Of course, capital is often acquired through the retention of earnings which incurs no out-of pocket financing cost. However, investors as a rule have no reason to accept a company earning less on profits retained than on new capital invested by them. The cost of common capital for companies A and B, assuming investors expected an 8.3 percent return ($8.30 for $100.00 market price), would be computed as follows:

Market price of common stock	$100.00
Less: 20% financing costs	20.00
Net proceeds to company	$ 80.00
Management's estimate of profit	$ 9.00
Investors' estimate of profit	$ 8.30

$$\text{Common cost} = \frac{\$ 8.30}{\$80.00} = 10.4\%$$

If the current earnings of Company A are $5.00, the stockholders are expecting a significant improvement in earnings potential to $8.30. If the current earnings of Company B are $10.00, the stockholders are expecting a decline in earnings to $8.30. For both companies, however, the cost of capital is the same, and each company's common stock is selling for $100.00 based on *investor* estimated profit of $8.30.

RELATIONSHIP OF BOOK VALUE TO MARKET VALUE

Company managers only have the capital available to them with which to earn a profit. They do not have the market value or price. But market value is used to determine cost of capital. To illustrate: Assume Company A has *only one share* with a book value of $75.00. It earns $8.30 for a return on investment (ROI) of 11.1 percent ($8.30 ÷ $75.00) on book value. Company A then sells one new share at the market price of $100.00 (disregard the financing costs for simplicity). Investors now expect total earnings of $16.60 ($8.30 per share × 2 shares) and total market value is $200.00.

BEFORE SELLING NEW SHARE

Earnings	$ 8.30	Earnings	$ 8.30
Book value	$75.00	Market value	$100.00
ROI	11.1%	Cost of capital	8.3%
		Price/earnings ratio	12.05

AFTER SELLING NEW SHARE

Earnings	$ 16.60	Earnings	$ 16.60
Book value	$175.00	Market value	$200.00
ROI	9.5%	Cost of capital	8.3%
		Price/earnings ratio	12.05

There has been no change in Company A's cost of capital as reflected by market value. However, the rate of return as measured by book value declines from 11.1 percent before the new share was sold to 9.5 percent after the new issue. However, the company is doing as well as it did before vis-a-vis its investors. Provided the new capital (or retained earnings) is invested at or above the cost of capital rate, the return on book value will not fall below the cost of capital rate.

DETERMINING NOXTON'S COST OF COMMON CAPITAL

Jones begins by establishing some benchmarks for cost of common capital. Because market prices are affected by many factors, average prices over a period of time will usually provide a more accurate relationship between price and earnings. He lists the average price, earnings, dividends, and dividend yields for the Dow-Jones Industrial Stocks for the last five years. The market results for these large, well-established companies are a useful benchmark. Financial managers outside the U.S. can obtain the same kinds of data about large firms in their countries. He also lists the yields on *prime* industrial bonds outstanding over this period.

MEASURES TO HELP DETERMINE COMMON CAPITAL COST

(Dow-Jones Industrial Stocks)

Year	Average Price	Earnings	Dividends	Dividend Yield	Industrial Prime Bonds
19X6	$ 950	$110.00	$ 47.75	5.00%	8.50%
19X5	895	89.10	45.80	5.51	7.80
19X4	999	96.72	41.40	4.12	8.23
19X3	823	75.66	37.46	4.39	8.61
19X2	718	99.04	37.72	6.12	8.42
Total	$4,385	$470.52	$210.13	25.14	41.56
5-year average	$ 877	$ 94.10	$ 42.03	5.03% (weighted)	8.31%

Using the five-year average, Jones computes the average cost of common capital:

Average price (5 years)	$877
Less: 10% financing cost	88
Net proceeds	$789
Average earnings	$ 94.10

$$\text{Cost of capital } \frac{\$\ 94.10}{\$789.00} = 11.9\%$$

He next divides average dividends of $42.03 by average earnings of $94.10 and gets a dividend payout ratio of 44.7 percent. Since the average dividend yield is 5.03 percent, the average earnings yield is 11.25 percent (5.03% ÷ .447), almost 3 percentage points higher than the average yield on industrial prime bonds of 8.31 percent. By including financing costs to obtain the equivalent cost of capital rate, the earnings yield of 11.25 percent becomes 12.5 percent (11.25% ÷ .90, which assumes for these large companies the lowest additional costs of financing as explained earlier).

THE GROWTH RATE APPROACH TO DETERMINE COST OF CAPITAL

Jones now computes the cost of capital based on the growth rate approach. He takes earnings figures from his previous measures shown on page 63:

19X6 earnings (estimated)	$110.00	
19X1 earnings (base year)	89.10	(not shown on page 63)
5-year growth ratio	1.2765	($110.00 ÷ $89.10)
Average compound annual growth rate	.0500	
Average dividend yield	.0503	
Total	.1003	

Cost of capital = 10.03 ÷ .90 = 11.14% (assume, as with previous illustration, 10% less than market value will be received as explained earlier)

Jones now has a range for cost of capital for the Dow-Jones Industrial Stocks of 11.14 percent to 12.5 percent for a benchmark.

CALCULATION OF COST OF COMMON CAPITAL FOR NOXTON AND COMPETITORS

He next examines Noxton's market performance as well as those of Excello and Arxco, competitors with similar product lines. If Noxton were a private company, market information would not be available and Jones would base his estimates of cost of capital on benchmarks such as competitors' results, growth rates, and/or public bond yields. In

	Noxton		Excello		Arxco	
	Average* Price	Per Share Earnings	Average* Price	Per Share Earnings	Average* Price	Per Share Earnings
19X6	$ 6.55	$ .82	$19.75	$ 2.70	$ 33.84	$ 4.35
19X5	6.25	.72	19.50	2.45	34.00	3.60
19X4	5.45	.66	17.75	2.10	29.50	3.25
19X3	5.25	.54	18.50	1.65	24.25	2.60
19X2	5.75	.57	18.80	1.60	25.60	2.10
Total	$29.25	$3.31	$94.30	$10.50	$147.19	$15.90
Average	$ 5.85	$ .66(A)	$18.86	$ 2.10(A)	$ 29.44	$ 3.18(A)
	80%† =	$4.68(B)	$15.09(B)†		$ 23.55(B)†	

(A) ÷ (B) = average share earnings ÷ reduced average price = % cost of capital

14.1% cost of capital   13.9% cost of capital   13.5% cost of capital
(Noxton)   (Excello)   (Arxco)

*Average of high and low in year.
†Average price reduced by 20% cost of financing for smaller, less well-known companies as explained on page 61.

Figure 19. Comparisons of cost of common capital

this example, however, the data are publicly available, and are shown in Figure 19.

Both Excello and Arxco exceed Noxton in return on book investment (see Figure 10). They are generally perceived as somewhat stronger companies. Jones therefore believes the market may assign a lower risk to them indicated by the slightly lower cost of capital.

Jones believes that the earnings yield approach to cost of capital (average earnings ÷ average market price) produces reasonable results for Noxton. Noxton's cost of common capital of 14.1 percent appears to be consistent with others in the industry. It exceeds the range for Dow-Jones Industrials by 1.6 to 3.0 percentage points. This also appears reasonable since *medium* grade bond rates have an average yield of 9.2 percent versus *prime* grade bond yield of 8.3 percent for a spread of 0.9 percentage points.

The 14.1 percent is also about 1.1 percentage points higher than the average return as measured by Standard & Poor's market index of

500 stocks over time. Since Noxton is a relatively small company, even among those included in this broader measure of the market, Jones believes that the relative spread among all the rates are reasonable.

He therefore concludes that 14.1 percent is representative of Noxton's cost of *common* capital. Since stock investors can only regard profits after tax, the 14.1 percent is the after-tax cost of common capital to Noxton.

At times the earning yield approach does not give reasonable results. This usually occurs when investors over the period expected higher or lower growth than actually resulted. When calculations result in unrealistically low or high costs of common capital, the reason can usually be determined by discussions with security analysts and others about investor attitudes and expectations. At such times the cost of capital should be estimated using benchmarks and spreads from bond yields.

THE DIVIDEND GROWTH MODEL

Jones then uses the dividend growth model to test the reasonableness of his 14.1 percent estimate. The formula is:

$$\text{Cost} = \frac{D}{P} + g$$

where "D" is the expected current year's dividend, "P" is the current price of the stock, and "g" is the investors' expected dividend growth rate.

Noxton's current stock price is $6.75 per share. The annual dividend is $.50. The dividend yield $\frac{(D)}{(P)}$ is thus 7.4 percent.

It is difficult to estimate "g"—the dividend growth rate. But Jones reasons that if the cost of common *is* 14.1 percent, the implied "g" is 6.7 percent (14.1% − 7.4% = 6.7%). Noxton's dividend growth rate has exceeded 6.7 percent in some years and fallen below in other years, but the rate appears to be a reasonable average.

In addition, he feels that since Noxton is currently paying out more than 50 percent of its earnings in dividends, the expected growth rate should tend to be slightly lower than the dividend yield of 7.4 percent (see page 60 illustration for Companies A and B). Therefore, he concludes that the dividend growth model does support his 14.1 percent cost of common capital estimate.

THE CAPITAL ASSET PRICING MODEL

Estimating the cost of common capital requires subjective judgments. However, the capital asset pricing model (CAPM) attempts to depict how investors actually price securities. The model has received a lot of attention in recent years in both the academic and corporate worlds.

CAPM provides a method for quantifying investment risk. Also, it makes it unnecessary to estimate a company's future growth rate or earnings. It is a useful technique that can complement other estimates of common capital cost.

The CAPM formula is:

$R = R_1 + \beta (R_m - R_1)$ where:

R = the stock's expected return (cost of common)

R_1 = the risk-free rate of return

β = the stock's beta (its variability in price relative to a market price index)

R_m = the expected return on the stock market as a whole

The risk-free rate of return (R_1) is the rate on government securities. Many analysts who use CAPM assign a risk premium ($R_m - R_1$) of 6 percent, which is the result of a long-term study of the average risk premium on 500 stocks.

A stock's beta (β) can be obtained from many investment firms if it is traded. Industry averages are also available which can help a private company estimate its beta.

However, Jones computes Noxton's beta using appropriate statistical methods. It is 1.2. (A beta of 1.0 indicates that the stock price fluctuates at the same rate as the market index.)

To estimate the cost of common using the CAPM, Jones simply plugs the appropriate numbers into the model. He uses the government's borrowing rate of 7.0 percent for the risk-free return.

Cost of Noxton's common $= 7.0 + 1.2(13.0 - 7.0) = 14.2\%$

Cost of capital is an estimate, and some analysts use three or four methods to compute it and then average the results. But in this example, the CAPM result is very close to 14.1 percent, and Jones decides to use 14.1 percent as Noxton's cost.

WEIGHTED AVERAGE COST OF CAPITAL

Jones now calculates Noxton's weighted average cost of all capital. He has the following pre-tax and after-tax costs available:

Long-term debt	9.50% or 4.94% after tax
Leases	10.90% or 8.67% after tax (10% residual)
Preferred stock	9.20% or 9.20% after tax
Common capital	14.10% or 14.10% after tax

Using the book capital available to Noxton at the end of 19X6, Jones constructs the following table:

		%	×	To Investor Rate	=	Investor Basis				After Tax*
Long-term debt	$2,500	31.3	×	.095	=	2.97	×	.52*	=	1.54%
Common capital	5,480	68.7	×	.141	=	9.69			=	9.69
Total capital	$7,980	100.0		—		12.66				11.23%

Note: 000 omitted.
*Tax rate of 48% assumed.

Jones uses the actual book ratio of long-term debt to total capital of 31.3 percent for weighting because he believes Noxton will continue to have this approximate ratio *in the future.* If Noxton planned to change the ratio, he would use the planned ratio rather than the actual ratio.

Noxton's after-tax weighted average cost of capital, then, is 11.23 percent which Jones rounds to 11.25 percent.

Because leasing is a possibility to Noxton, Jones also calculates cost of capital with $235,000 of leases (the maximum for the company's debt to total capital ratio of 33.3 percent).

		%	×	To Investor Rate	=	Investor Basis			After Tax
Long-term debt	$2,500	30.4	×	.095	=	2.89	× .52* =		1.50%*
Leases	235	2.9	×	.109	=	.32			.25†
Common capital	5,480	66.7	×	.141	=	9.40			9.40
Total	$8,215	100.00		—		12.61			11.15%

Note: 000 omitted.
* Tax rate of 48% assumed.
† After-tax cost of lease of 8.67% × .029, which is the % of leases to total capital and leases.

The after-tax cost of leasing is lower than the cost of common capital. As a result, the weighted average cost of total capital decreases slightly. A company's cost of capital can normally be reduced by borrowing up to a point where lenders begin to impose severely high interest rates. At that point common investors will also assign higher costs because of risk. Usually for industrial companies, this occurs when debt reaches 55 to 60 percent of total capital. Therefore, prudent capital management suggests that debt levels be kept within comfortable limits (about 33 percent for Noxton) and normal ranges accepted by the financial community.

V

How to Calculate and Plan for Adequate Return on Investment

Profit is not a complete measure of a company's performance. It must be related to the amount of capital used to produce it. As risk increases, the amount of capital required to achieve a given amount of profit decreases.

The table below shows various kinds of investments ranked according to risk. It illustrates the relationships among them according to risk, rate of return, and capital required to produce $100 profit at that rate:

Investment Risk Low to High	Market Rate of Return	Capital Required for $100 profit ($100 ÷ market rate)
U.S. government bonds	8.25%	$1,212
Prime industrial bonds	8.50	1,176
Medium grade industrial bonds	9.20	1,087
Noxton—long-term notes	9.50	1,052
Dow-Jones Industrial stocks	11.90	840
Noxton—common stock	14.10	709

Market prices and therefore rates of return for these various investments are determined by many factors: the general price level, business conditions, profits, the particular industry and company outlook, competition, company and management reputation, psychological and speculative attitudes, and the like. Rates of return that are determined in the marketplace reflect the risks perceived by investors. They set the potential reward levels for those who wish to assume them.

COST OF CAPITAL AS THE STANDARD TO MEASURE PERFORMANCE

Jones has compared Noxton's return on book capital to other companies in the industry (see Figure 10). He knows that Noxton gets better results than some and not as good as others. Some executives use the results of other companies in the industry to set their own objectives. However, while one company may do better than another, that does not mean that it is meeting the standards of investors. For example, an entire industry may be declining because of technology changes or consumer preferences. Therefore, comparison to other companies may mislead management.

Cost of capital is the correct standard for measuring performance. Companies which earn their cost of capital or more over a period of time will be judged superior to those which do not. Their products are likely to be judged superior and be produced and delivered efficiently. Therefore, performance should be measured against cost of capital.

THE BASES FOR RETURN ON INVESTMENT

Jones has computed Noxton's 19X6 return on total book capital invested at 8.8 percent. (See pages 28 and 29, adjusted net income to total capital.) This rate uses capital as a base. It relates directly to cost of capital.

But return on investment can be stated with a different base, for example, assets. Noxton's net income for 19X6 divided by total assets at the beginning of 19X6 is 5.8 percent. Some managers use cash flow (net profit plus depreciation) divided by total assets plus the depreciation reserve. This method of calculating ROI would produce a 9.0 percent return for Noxton.

Assets as a base, rather than capital, may be useful *within* a company that operates divisions/departments as profit centers. Their managers are often responsible for meeting return on investment objectives. It is usually easier to determine the value of assets under a division manager's control than to allocate a portion of the total capital of the company to the division.

When a rate of return is stated, therefore, it is important to know *how* it is computed. Noxton's rates of 8.8, 5.8 and 9.0 percent are all valid as defined. It is equally important to know how they relate to cost of capital.

HOW TO USE COST OF CAPITAL TO DETERMINE WHAT PROFITS SHOULD BE

Noxton's weighted average cost of capital after tax is 11.25 percent as calculated by Jones in the preceding Section. Noxton earned 8.8 percent after tax on total book capital in 19X6. Jones can therefore determine what the results *should have been* based on cost of capital.

While the cost of capital was determined on the mix of capital, long-term debt and common stock at the *end* of fiscal year 19X6, there is no significant change in the rate or results if that cost is now applied to the capital at the *beginning* of 19X6. Jones plans to compute Noxton's cost of capital once a year in the future. He will also compute it whenever there is a *major* change in the composition of capital from new financing. The results of his analysis show:

NET AFTER TAX BASIS

	Cost of Capital	Actual
Total capital available beginning fiscal 19X6	$7,755,000	$7,755,000
Rate of return	11.25%	8.8%
Total capital × rate	872,000	680,000
Less: Interest expense after tax	124,000*	105,000
Net income	$ 748,000	$ 575,000

*Based on an interest cost of 9.5%.

Actual net income was $173,000 less than income based on cost of capital ($748,000 − $575,000 = $173,000). This comparison indicates that a profit gap exists that management should attempt to close. Areas to focus on to improve income include prices, market share, costs, new products, capital investments, and increased efficiency.

Managers should attempt to get the best results. Realistic goals well above cost of capital may be attainable. Cost of capital is not a ceiling. It is a floor. It should guide business decisions to obtain optimum results.

RATE OF RETURN ON BOOK CAPITAL

While the calculation of cost of capital is based on market values, financial managers apply it to book value in practice.

The book value of long-term debt that appears on a company's balance sheet is usually stated realistically.

However, the value of the common capital as stated in the balance sheet is sometimes open to question. For instance, a company may be very profitable based largely on franchise or licensing agreements, the capitalized values of which are not included in the capital accounts on the financial statements.

In such a case, applying the cost of capital rate to a very low book capital could produce a profit goal that would be lower than actual past results. In such instances, managers can adjust book capital for setting profit goals. For most companies, however, the financial statement common capital can be used with confidence.

If managers can earn more than the cost of capital rate on all *new* projects (with capital realistically valued at the time of investment) and/or increase the rate of return on existing book capital by being more efficient, they will ensure an optimum value for the common stock.

RETURN ON INVESTMENT FOR PROFIT CENTERS

Return on investment can be used to appraise the performance of division/department managers of profit centers. If each subordinate manager focuses on the same objective, that will help the company to achieve its total return on investment objective.

There are two benefits from using a return on investment standard. First, proposed profit plans can be measured against a reliable guide and, if not acceptable, revisions can be made. Second, manager performance can be assessed against the actual results produced. Return on investment can also be used to evaluate business segments, either geographically or by product line. And when return on investment standards are not met, management can search for solutions.

Division/department managers, even those operating profit centers, are seldom completely autonomous. Normally their capital budgets must be reviewed with senior management. And at times projects may be assigned to them that will not contribute to profitability.

Setting return on investment standards for division/department managers, therefore, must be done with care. And, actual results should be reviewed, considering the real contributions by them. Furthermore, they should be evaluated by more than the ROI standard. Share of market, sales volume, costs, and other criteria should also be used. When return on investment is overemphasized, some managers, to improve ROI today, may postpone needed investments that would improve long-term profitability. Or they might cut costs that could hurt future years' results.

ALLOCATING RETURN ON INVESTMENT STANDARDS

Once the overall standard for ROI has been set, then portions of it can be allocated to profit centers or to major product lines. Managers should be encouraged to recommend new investment projects as long as their profitability exceeds the cost of capital rate.

The total objective is not to achieve the largest rate of return today, but to maximize it in the long run.

Subordinate managers can be encouraged to propose or accept projects that have lower than their current rate of return providing the return is at least as great as the cost of capital rate. One approach is to use *residual profit* as a performance criterion. Residual profit is illustrated by Jones in the following analysis of profitability of Noxton's major product lines. Noxton does not have profit centers, but Jones wants to apply cost of capital standards to product lines to assist management in improving overall profitability.

COST OF CAPITAL APPLIED TO PRODUCT LINES

Noxton has two major product lines—industrial and residential. Each has a sales manager who reports to the general sales manager and a manager of production who reports to the manager of manufacturing.

In Figure 20, Jones lists Noxton's total *assets* at the beginning of fiscal 19X6. He allocates amounts of assets to each of the product lines. With assets such as accounts receivable and inventory, the allocation is simple because the accounting records show the amounts.

The allocation method for cash and certain other items is arbitrary, but normally the results are realistic. For instance, Jones allocates long-term assets on the basis of square feet of factory space used in the production process. If the value of machinery was significantly different between the products, however, Jones could allocate the values of the major machines first and then allocate the remainder of the long-term assets on the basis of factory space used for each product line.

Jones next allocates the income statement items. The sales and cost of sales amounts are available from accounting records. Selling and administrative expenses are allocated on the basis of the respective ratio of sales of each product line to total sales. Significant differences between product lines in the number of salespeople, promotion, or advertising, could be considered in the allocation process, but are not in Noxton's case.

He next takes the cost of capital net income as it should have been for 19X6 of $748,000, calculated as shown on page 72, and divides it by the total assets of $9,945,000 at the beginning of 19X6 to obtain a rate of return on *assets* of 7.5 percent. He applies 7.5 percent to the allocated assets of each product line to arrive at a cost of capital net income of $468,000 for industrial products and $279,000 for residential. Jones deducts the cost of capital net income from the allocated net income to obtain the *residual income* for each product line.

Residual income is negative for Noxton because the company is not earning at the cost of capital rate, and it is negative for each of the product lines. However, industrial products net income almost breaks even versus cost of capital. But residential products net income is $157,000 under, showing that this product line is much less profitable versus cost of capital. Jones will bring the attention of top executives to residential products' low profitability and assist them to improve it. The allocation

Assets Employed	Total Noxton Fiscal Year 19X5	Method of Allocation	Industrial Products	Residential Products
Cash	$ 900	*	$ 565	$ 335
Accounts receivable	1,220	actual	818	402
Inventory	3,792	actual	2,220	1,572
Other assets	40	*	23	17
Long-term assets	3,993	square feet used	2,607	1,386
Total assets	$9,945	—	$6,233	$3,712
Income				
Sales	$14,415	actual	$9,820	$4,595
Cost of sales	11,775	actual	7,905	3,870
Selling and administrative expense	1,325	% sales	903	422
Other	215	% sales	146	69
Profit before tax	1,100	—	866	234
Income tax	525	% profit	413	112
Net income	$ 575	—	$ 453	$ 122

Cost of capital net income ÷ total assets = cost of capital rate of return on total assets

$748 (page 72)   ÷ $9,945   =   7.5%

Net income (A)	$ 575		$ 453	$ 122
Cost of capital ROI 7.5% × total assets (B)	748		468	279
Residual income (A) − (B)	$ (173)		$ (15)	$ (157)

Note: 000 omitted.
* Based on ratio to receivables, inventory, and long-term assets.

Figure 20. Allocation of cost of capital standards to product lines

process can be carried into major subproduct groups and even to individual products, although it becomes increasingly difficult to allocate assets.

Residual income solves the conflict that often develops when managers of profit centers are held responsible for both return on investment and contribution to profit. As long as the profitability on a new investment exceeds the cost of capital rate, residual income will increase. The manager's rate of return on his total investment may decrease, depending on the actual level of profit, but the added profits contribute meaningfully to the total company objective.

RESIDUAL INCOME—SUBPRODUCT GROUPS

Because the analysis in Figure 20 shows a problem of low profitability in the residential products line, Jones continues the analysis as shown in Figure 21. Two subproduct groups are circuit breakers and temperature controls. He allocates the assets of residential products to them following the same procedures as before. However, for long-term assets he allocates the value of the major machines used in producing the circuit breakers and temperature controls, and overhead costs which are supplied by the controller. He does not allocate income taxes in this example because usually rates are affected by actions at the corporate level. Also, losses in a product group would require assigning a tax credit.

Jones takes the $279,000 income after tax based on cost of capital for residential products (Figure 20) and divides by 1.000 minus the tax rate of .477 or .523 to arrive at the $535,000 pretax profit for the total residential product group. Dividing $535,000 by the group assets of $3,712,000 gives him a rate of 14.4 percent, which he then applies to the assets allocated to the subgroups to arrive at cost of capital pretax profits. Subtracting these amounts from allocated profits results in obtaining the residual pretax profits for each subgroup product, $226,000 for circuit breakers and $75,000 for temperature controls. The residual income amounts are negative for both products.

Assets Employed	Total Residential Products	Method of Allocation	Circuit Breakers	Temperature Controls
Cash	$ 335	*	$ 203	$ 132
Accounts receivable	402	actual	202	200
Inventory	1,572	actual	922	650
Other assets	17	*	11	6
Long-term assets	1,386	†	911	475
Total assets	$3,712	—	$2,249	$1,463
Income				
Sales	$4,595	actual	$2,405	$2,190
Cost of sales	3,870	actual	2,050	1,820
Selling and administrative expense	422	% sales	221	201
Other	69	% sales	36	33
Profit before tax	$ 234	—	$ 98	$ 136

Cost of capital profit before tax ÷ total assets = cost of capital rate of return before tax on total assets

$279 (Figure 20) ÷ (1.000 − .477)‡ ÷ $3,712 = 14.4%

Profit before tax (A)	$ 234	$ 98	$ 136
Cost of capital ROI before tax 14.4% × total assets (B)	535	324	211
Residual income before tax (A) − (B)	$ (301)	$ (226)	$ (75)

Note: 000 omitted.
* Based on ratio to receivables, inventory, and long-term assets.
† Based on major machines used plus overhead allocation.
‡ Cost of capital profit before tax is calculated by dividing the after-tax profit by 1.000 − tax rate of .477.

Figure 21. Allocation of cost of capital standards to products

HOW TO CALCULATE PRICE INCREASES TO MEET COST OF CAPITAL NEEDS

If circuit breakers could earn $226,000 more pretax, it would meet Noxton's cost of capital goals. Jones continues the analysis on circuit breakers using unit costs and total costs as shown in the table below:

CIRCUIT BREAKERS

Units sold 19X6—14,500	Unit	Total (000 omitted)
Sales	$165.50	$2,405
Cost of sales		
Direct labor	26.50	385
Materials	69.51	1,010
Overhead and other	45.06	655
Gross margin	24.43	355
Selling and administration	17.67*	257
Profit before tax	$ 6.76	$ 98

*Based on % of sales.

Jones can compute what the unit profit before tax should be based on cost of capital. Dividing $324,000 (the circuit breaker cost of capital income before tax from Figure 21) by units sold of 14,500, he obtains $22.34. If the unit price can be increased by enough to yield an additional $15.58 ($22.34 − $6.76), or 9.4 percent, circuit breakers will meet the cost of capital standard.

HOW TO CALCULATE SALES VOLUME INCREASES TO MEET COST OF CAPITAL NEEDS

Because some costs are fixed, an increase in sales volume will also improve results. Fixed costs (obtained from the controller) total $474,000 for both manufacturing overhead and selling and administrative expenses. Jones can calculate the volume increase needed, at current prices, to meet cost of capital. He computes variable expenses of $1,833,000 by deducting from total expenses of $2,307,000 the fixed expenses of $474,000. Thus, variable expenses are 76.2 percent of total sales.

Total sales would have to be large enough to cover variable expenses plus $474,000 of fixed expenses plus $324,000 of pretax profit. Jones arrives at the required sales figure by dividing $474,000 + $324,000 ($798,000) by 1 − .762 (.762 is the percent of variable expense to sales). This calculation gives a sales value of $3,353,000. Dividing the required sales value ($3,353,000) by the current unit price of $165.50 results in a required sales *volume* of 20,260 units, about 40 percent above the recent 14,500 unit level.

Managers often believe that volume increases can offset the need for price increases. Normally, however, as this Noxton example illustrates, a substantial increase in sales volume is necessary if used to improve profitability instead of a needed price increase. Of course, cost reductions will help profit also. But in this instance it does not appear that unit cost reductions alone can close the gap between what profits are and what they should be in relation to cost of capital.

When competition does not permit prices to be increased, a company must rely on sales volume increases and/or cost reduction measures to improve results. If the situation does not improve, management should consider replacing circuit breakers with another product which will earn its cost of capital. Such decisions are the most difficult ones that top executives must make.

DISCOUNTED CASH FLOW RATE OF RETURN

The discounted cash flow rate of return (DCF) represents the interest rate that causes the annual cash flows over a period of time to discount to a zero present value. DCF is based on the principle that a dollar received sometime in the future is worth less to an investor than a dollar received today.

Figure 22 shows the annual cash flows and net present values for a hypothetical investment of $1,000.00 with a five-year life. The interest rate (the DCF rate) that discounts the cash flows to zero is 10 percent. As can be seen under the heading "Investment Amortization Schedule" in Figure 22, the 10 percent rate amortizes the $1,000.00 investment to zero over the five-year period. The DCF rate is often referred to as the internal rate of return (IRR).

Unfortunately, DCF rates of return are difficult to compute, particularly in complex projects. They involve trial and error when done by hand. But there are computer programs which compute the DCF rate quickly. Small programmable calculators are also available.

Figure 23 shows a worksheet that contains trial discount factors for various rates of return. With a little practice, an analyst can estimate the DCF rate with reasonable accuracy, discount the cash flows using the factors for interest rates lower and higher than the estimate and then interpolate. The result is normally within an acceptable range of error.

For example, the annual cash flows of $263.79 for the hypothetical $1,000 project in Figure 22 have been entered under the heading "cash flow" in the worksheet in Figure 23. These cash flows have been discounted on the "Trial DCF Rate of Return Calculation" at 5 percent and 15 percent. The net present value of the cash flows discounted at 5 percent is positive, meaning the DCF rate is higher than 5 percent. The total of the net present value of the cash flows discounted at 15 percent is negative, meaning the DCF rate is lower than 15 percent. Through interpolation using the formula shown below, the DCF rate of return for the project is 10.5 percent (compared to an actual of 10.0 percent). Normally the error through interpolation will not exceed .2 percent if the range between the rates is 5 percent or less.

Interpolation formula

Low discount rate +
   (high discount rate − low discount rate) ×
$$\frac{\text{high present value} - \text{investment}}{\text{high present value} - \text{low present value}} = \text{DCF rate}$$

$$5\% + (15\% - 5\%) \times \frac{(142.21)}{(257.72)} - 10.5\%$$

The DCF rate of return on a project can be compared directly to a company's cost of capital rate. This is not true for book method rates of return. For instance, if the company's cost of capital after tax is 10 percent, the 10 percent project described in Figure 22 would be an acceptable project.

The book rates of return, however, are 6.4 percent on total capital

Year	Cash Income (1)	Depreciation (2)	Income Tax† (3)	Net Profit (4)	Net Cash Flow (2) + (4) (5)	10% Discount Factors (6)	Present Value at 10% (5) × (6)
0*	—	—	—	—	$(1,000.00)	1.000	$(1,000.00)
1	$ 327.58	$ 200.00	$ 63.79	$ 63.79	263.79	.909	239.79
2	327.58	200.00	63.79	63.79	263.79	.826	218.01
3	327.58	200.00	63.79	63.79	263.79	.751	198.19
4	327.58	200.00	63.79	63.79	263.79	.683	180.17
5	327.58	200.00	63.79	63.79	263.79	.621	163.79
Total	$1,637.90	$1,000.00	$318.95	$318.95	$ 318.95		$(.05)‡

INVESTMENT AMORTIZATION SCHEDULE

Year	Principal Outstanding Beginning of Year	Annual Payment	10% Interest on Principal	Principal Retired in Year	Principal Outstanding End of Year
1	$1,000.00	$ 263.79	$100.00	$163.79	$836.21
2	836.21	263.79	83.62	180.17	656.04
3	656.04	263.79	65.60	198.19	457.85
4	457.85	263.79	45.79	218.00	239.85
5	239.85	263.79	23.99	239.80	.05‡
Total	—	$1,318.95	$319.00	$999.95	—

* Investment of $1,000.00 considered to take place in year 0.
† Income tax rate assumed—50%
‡ Difference due to rounding. Should equal 0.

Figure 22. Discounted cash flow rate of return

invested (average profit of $63.79 divided by $1,000.00) and 12.8 percent on *average* capital invested ($63.79 divided by $500.00). Using the first book measure, the project would be rejected if 10 percent were the minimum acceptable rate. It would be approved if average capital outstanding, the other book measure, were used.

The book rate of return methods do not consider the time value of money. They treat a dollar received in year 1 the same as a dollar received in year 5 or 10 in terms of value.

Book rates of return also reflect book depreciation rates. For example, in Figure 22, depreciation of $200 is taken for book purposes each year (affecting the reported net profit) while the investment amortization schedule shows that the principal is retired by $163.79 in the first year, by $180.17 in the second year, increasing to $239.80 in year 5. The total depreciation of $1,000.00 equals the total principal retired over the life of the investment, but the *timing* is different. When considering a company with many projects underway, the differences between total book depreciation in any one year and *total* investment principal amortized will normally average out. Book rates of return on investment for a *total company* will therefore be a valid measure, but they're not valid for single projects.

However, if a company is not investing in new depreciable assets at a reasonable level, the average age of the assets in use will increase toward their depreciable life. Therefore, the book rates of return even for a *total* company may not be a valid measure of earning capability if the assets are nearing the end of their useful life.

If the project shown in Figure 22 had a DCF rate of return of 9 percent, it should *not* be approved against a 10 percent cost of capital standard. However, if the average book method were used, the project's rate would be 11.4 percent, still suggesting that it was acceptable. Book method rates of return are *poor* measures of profitability when comparing various projects against each other or cost of capital standards. This subject will be discussed further in the Section on evaluating capital investments.

COST OF CAPITAL STANDARDS SHOULD CONSIDER RISK

Noxton's cost of capital rate of 11.25 percent after tax is the minimum acceptable rate of return for any project where profit is the major cri-

Investment: Capital facilities $1,000.00
           Expenses (after tax)   —
           Working capital   —
           Total $1,000.00

CASH FLOW

TRIAL DCF RATE OF RETURN CALCULATION

Year	Profit After Tax	Depreciation	Other	Total	5% Discount		10% Discount		15% Discount		20% Discount		25% Discount	
					Factor	Present Value	Factor	Present Value	Factor	Present Value	Factor	Present Value	Factor	Present Value
0	—	—	—	—	1.000	(1,000.00)	1.000		1.000	(1,000.00)	1.000		1.000	
1	63.79	200.00	—	263.79	.952	251.13	.909		.870	229.50	.833		.800	
2	63.79	200.00	—	263.79	.907	239.26	.826		.756	199.43	.694		.640	
3	63.79	200.00	—	263.79	.864	227.91	.751		.658	173.57	.579		.512	
4	63.79	200.00	—	263.79	.823	217.10	.683		.572	150.89	.482		.410	
5	63.79	200.00	—	263.79	.784	206.81	.621		.497	131.10	.402		.328	
6					.746		.564		.432		.335		.262	
7					.711		.513		.376		.279		.210	
8					.677		.467		.327		.233		.168	
9					.645		.424		.284		.194		.134	
10					.614		.386		.247		.162		.107	

TRIAL DCF RATE OF RETURN CALCULATION

	CASH FLOW				5% Discount		10% Discount		15% Discount		20% Discount		25% Discount	
Year	Profit After Tax	Depre-ciation	Other	Total	Factor	Present Value	Factor	Present Value	Factor	Present Value	Factor	Present Value	Factor	Present Value
11					.585		.350		.215		.135		.086	
12					.557		.319		.187		.112		.069	
13					.530		.290		.163		.093		.055	
14					.505		.263		.141		.078		.044	
15					.481		.239		.123		.065		.035	
16					.458		.218		.107		.054		.028	
17					.436		.198		.093		.045		.023	
18					.416		.180		.081		.038		.018	
19					.396		.164		.070		.031		.014	
20					.377		.149		.061		.026		.012	
Total	318.95	1,000.00	—	1,318.75	—	142.21	—		—	(115.51)	—		—	

Interpolation: Low discount rate + $\left(\dfrac{\text{high discount rate}}{-\text{ low discount rate}}\right) \times \dfrac{\text{high present value } - \text{ investment}}{\text{high present value } - \text{ low present value}}$ = DCF rate

$$5\% + (10\%) \times \frac{142.21}{257.72} = 10.5\%$$

Figure 23. Worksheet for calculating DCF rates of return

terion for approval. However, managers must approve some expenditures which have little measurable profit. For instance, capital may need to be invested to resurface the parking lot. Capital expenditures that have no measurable profit may need to be made to improve plant safety or pollution control.

Also, projects that do have profit as an objective use assumptions and estimates. Results might be poorer than expected. Therefore, most financial managers increase the cost of capital rate for judging whether new investments should be made. As a safety factor, Jones increases the cost of capital rate after tax for Noxton by 5 percentage points to 16.25 percent. Capital expenditures that expand the current business and product lines normally have less risk than new products or new business ventures. They can be judged against the 16.25 percent standard for Noxton. New products, however, are more risky and would be judged against a higher rate. Jones selects 20 percent for such new products.

Setting these standards requires judgment and realistic appraisals of risk. For instance, Noxton has no international operations. If it was considering a new venture in a foreign country, the risk would be higher than a domestic new product or venture. A standard of 30 percent or more, depending on conditions in the particular country, would be more appropriate than the 20 percent standard Jones sets for domestic new projects.

Risks vary among different product lines or divisions in a company. For example, Noxton's industrial products may be less risky than residential products. Demand may be easier to forecast, the company may be dealing with professional buyers, product specifications may be well defined, etc. If there are competing companies in one product and not the other, estimating their cost of capital may provide guidelines for assigning different cost of capital standards to product lines within a company.

In profit center management, the managers should also perform against standards that reflect the risk of their particular operations. For example, the manager of a foreign division may earn an actual rate of return of 18 percent as compared to a manager of a stable, domestic division who earns 13 percent. The risk of the foreign operation may be assessed at a 20 percent cost of capital rate of return, however, while the risk of the domestic operation is assessed at 11 percent. The domestic manager is getting results above his cost of capital rate while the foreign manager needs to improve his results.

COST OF CAPITAL PROFIT GOALS

Cost of capital rates can be used to establish minimum company profit goals. The objective, however, should be to earn *more* than cost of capital. For setting profit goals (as opposed to new project profit goals), Jones will recommend to management that cost of capital plus 2 percent be used as a minimum. The minimum profit goal rate for Noxton, therefore, will be 13.25 percent, 11.25 percent + 2.00 percent.

Companies may increase profits by acquiring other companies. Cost of capital standards should also be applied in evaluating acquisitions. However, the acquiring company's standard should not be applied.

For example, if Noxton considers buying a company that has a cost of capital of 13.50 percent, the risk is 13.50 percent; it is not Noxton's cost of capital of 11.25 percent. To set a standard, Jones would take the target company's cost of capital rate of 13.5 percent, add 2 percent for a higher profit goal, 5 percent for risks associated in an acquisition, and set 20.5 percent as the cost of capital standard rate necessary to go through with the acquisition. If the estimated DCF rate of return on the acquisition project was 15 percent, which might seem attractive to Noxton because it is higher than Noxton's own rate, the acquisition should probably not be consummated. The potential profit is too low considering the risks.

PROJECT RATE OF RETURN—NO LEVERAGE

Figure 22 shows the cash flows for a project with a $1,000.00 investment and life of five years. The DCF rate is 10 percent. The 10 percent is the rate of return for this particular project. If $500.00 of the required investment were borrowed at 10 percent and the cash flows were restated to include interest after tax and loan repayments, the DCF rate of return would appear to increase to 15 percent on the reduced $500.00 investment. The DCF rate increases because the investment is reduced by a larger percentage than the cash flows whenever leverage is introduced. The table on page 88 illustrates:

Year	Income	Depreciation	Interest	Tax	Profit	Loan Repayment	Cash Flow
No Leverage with $1000.00 Investment							
1	$327.58	$200.00	—	$63.79	$63.79	—	$263.79
Leverage with $500.00 Investment							
1	$327.58	$200.00	$50.00	$38.79	$38.79	$81.90	$156.89

Investment has been reduced by 50 percent ($1,000.00 to $500.00) by leverage from borrowing, while cash flow in year 1 is reduced by only 40.5 percent ($263.79 − $156.89 = $106.90).

If the cash flows in the leverage case are calculated for five years into the future, they will gradually decrease as the annual loan payments (which are not tax deductible) increase. However, because of the time value of money, the DCF rate will be 15 percent. Any DCF rate desired can be computed by varying the amount of leverage. For instance, 100 percent leverage would result in an infinite DCF rate of return.

In all cases, however, the *project* has a basic profit rate of 10 percent, no more, no less. If cost of capital is 11.25 percent, a 10 percent project should not be approved. Leveraging the project to 15 percent does not improve it versus cost of capital. That would confuse the source of capital (the cost of which is the standard) with the use of capital (the basic profit). If all projects were leveraged to give them acceptable DCFs, the company's debt to total capital ratio would rise to levels that would soon cause substantial increases in cost of capital because both lenders and common stock investors would demand exorbitant interest rates for the risks involved.

When projects contain built-in financing, for example, a property is to be purchased with an attractive mortgage, the interest expense should be removed from cash flows and the total investment, including the mortgage, should be used to assess the profit rate of the project against cost of capital.

Noxton's weighted average cost of capital rate is 11.25 percent *after tax*. If a project on an unleveraged basis earns exactly 11.25 percent after tax, it will just satisfy the firm's lenders and common stockholders.

VI

How to Evaluate Long-Term Capital Investments

Capital investment in plant and equipment, unlike that in receivables and inventory, normally takes years to turn over. A company must live with its decisions on investments in long-term assets for long periods of time. Therefore, effective planning and control of such investments is crucial for orderly, profitable growth.

Capital investment planning starts with setting long-term goals for sales, production, and profits. Plans are developed which give the operating managers guidelines to make investment proposals to achieve the goals.

Most companics ask managers to prepare specific investment proposals each year. These are reviewed by senior management for consistency with long and short-term goals for justification, profitability, and so on. Approved projects form the company's capital budget for the coming year. Authorization to spend money, however, is usually not given when the budget is approved. Each investment of any size is subjected to a more detailed review during the budget year before senior management gives authorization to commit funds.

FRAMEWORK FOR CAPITAL INVESTMENT

Three basic questions need to be answered in budgeting capital for long-term investment:

1. How much money is needed?
2. How much money is available?
3. How can the available money best be allocated to the various projects?

The emphasis in evaluating capital investment opportunities should be *new* capital investment and *future* profit. Thus, investing in long-term assets involves uncertainty. Evaluation requires judgment and analytical skill. Estimates are required for future sales volumes, prices, and costs. The quality of these estimates is crucial to get the best combination of investments to improve the company's growth and profitability.

When possible, investment alternatives should be developed and evaluated. At times the alternative may be to do nothing, or to postpone investment. But a continuing policy of postponing profitable investment will lead to stagnation.

THE FOUR CAPITAL EXPENDITURE CATEGORIES

The first category is replacement. These are expenditures made to replace existing assets with similar ones. Cost savings often justify replacement expenditures.

For example, Noxton's production managers have wanted four new machines for several years but funds to buy them have not been available. The new machines are more efficient and will reduce labor, materials handling and maintenance costs. Such savings are relatively easy to estimate and the risk that they won't be achieved is relatively low.

Noxton's management took the investment alternative to defer the expenditures and to accept the higher costs. Of course, when a machine essential for production becomes unusable, it must be replaced. This is not the case at Noxton. Noxton's management has now included replacement of four machines in the capital budget for 19X7.

CAPITAL EXPENDITURES FOR EXPANSION

The investments in new equipment or plant expand production capacity. Their justification is future increases in sales and profits.

The alternative is not to expand and accept the loss of future sales and market share. Because estimates of future sales and profits are always uncertain, more risk is involved with this category of capital expenditure than with replacement investments. The cost of not expanding, however, can be even greater.

CAPITAL EXPENDITURES FOR PRODUCTS

Expenditures to improve existing products are justified to maintain or increase existing sales and market share. When competitors improve products, failure to follow can result in lower sales and market share. Conversely, the company that leads competitors in product improvement usually gets increased sales and market share.

This category of capital investment also includes extending the product line with similar products. Because of experience with similar products, managers usually can estimate future sales, market share, and costs with almost the same confidence as with existing products.

In addition, there are investments to add completely new types of products. These involve the greatest risk because new skills must often be learned in production. Moreover, there is more uncertainty about sales volume and price for new types of products.

STRATEGIC CAPITAL EXPENDITURES

It is usually difficult to quantify the effects of strategic investments although they are often considered necessary to carry on or expand the business and to reach long-term goals. For example, a company may decide it wants to own half of its distribution outlets. While the long-term effects are desirable because ownership contributes to operating independence, the start-up investments may be high in relation to the short-term profits.

However, there are often alternatives available within this category. While a proposed investment may not meet quantitative profit standards, investment in one city, for example, ownership of a distribution outlet, may cost less than in another when measured by a cost of capital standard.

There are also investments that *must* be made. An airline, for example, invests in safety and redundant flight equipment. There is no reasonable alternative.

HOW TO ANALYZE A CAPITAL BUDGET

Noxton's long-term goals are:

1. Increase sales volume 50 percent in the next five years.
2. Continue to produce a quality product at competitive cost.
3. Improve earnings per share by an average of 10 percent per year.

The specific objectives for the coming year of 19X7 are to increase sales by 15 percent and earnings per share by 13 percent. E.J. Carlson, Noxton's president, asked managers during the fourth quarter of 19X6 to submit proposals for capital investments in 19X7 to achieve these objectives. Senior executives eliminated some of the proposals during their review of the budget because of obvious low profitability, insufficient justification, and other reasons.

The approved budget for 19X7 totals $397,500. This compares to $300,000 in 19X6 ($200,000 actually invested).

Carlson has asked Jones to review the 19X7 approved budget in light of the forecast availability of funds, to make recommendations as to Noxton's capability to finance the projects, and to rank the individual investments in order of their profit contribution to assist management in its decisions on allocating funds.

STARTING THE CAPITAL BUDGET ANALYSIS

Jones first summarizes Noxton's 19X7 approved capital budget as shown following:

Project No.	Description	Capital Amount	Justification
X7-1	New control system for temperature regulation	$ 40,000	Increased sales and higher market share
X7-2 X7-3	Vacuum forming equipment	90,000	Increased sales Increased capacity
X7-4 X7-5 X7-6 X7-7	Four new machines to replace existing machines and improve efficiency	100,000	Cost savings
X7-8	Warehouse	105,000	Cost savings
X7-9	Cafeteria equipment	20,000	Employee relations
X7-10	Office equipment (various)	2,500	Replacement
X7-11	Automotive equipment	10,000	Replacement
	Contingency	30,000	
	Total	$397,500	

After reviewing the list he decides that projects X7-1 through X7-8 lend themselves to discounted cash flow (DCF) analysis. Project X7-10, office equipment, is to replace several unusable typewriters. The cafeteria project X7-9 and automotive equipment project X7-11 (replacement of a car) do not have measurable economic justifications.

Jones discusses price, sales volume, and cost assumptions for the projects with the appropriate operating managers. He then calculates the DCF rates of return so that he can rank the projects according to their estimated profit contribution to Noxton.

THE CASH FLOW PROFILE

Project X7-1 is a new energy conserving temperature control system for multistory buildings. The engineering department spent $35,000 in 19X6 in developing the product and, because of favorable test results, the department plans to spend an additional $25,000 in 19X7. Machinery for parts manufacturing for the product will require a capital investment of $40,000 as shown in the budget. The justification for the project is higher sales and improved market share.

Jones learns from the sales manager that the price of the new product cannot exceed $15,000 because of the competition. He forecasts that Noxton can sell 20 units in the first year (19X8) and 50 units a year thereafter. Unit costs of manufacturing the product are estimated at $12,000. Management also believes that Noxton must recover its costs and make a profit within a five-year period because new, more efficient systems will be developed during that time.

Jones prepares a cash flow profile for the project as shown in Figure 24. The profile enables management to see the income/expenses and cash flows by year. Because DCF rates of return are calculated using *future* cash flows, Jones does not include the research and development cost of $35,000 incurred in 19X6.

Under the income/expenses section of the profile, Jones enters the sales revenue, manufacturing, and other costs. For depreciation he enters Noxton's method of depreciation actually used for tax purposes, sum of the years digits. The income tax entries reflect the statutory rates and the actual cash outlays for taxes as and when they are expected to be made. A statutory rate of 50 percent has been used which covers both Federal and local taxes on income.

Under the cash flow section, Jones enters the profit after tax, the depreciation, and the cash outlay for equipment. Introducing a new product often requires an investment in working capital for inventory and receivables. Jones includes a total of $200,000 for working capital. The working capital, of course, will be recovered when the project ends and is shown as a cash inflow in the fifth year.

After completing the cash flow profile, Jones calculates the DCF rate of return. He discounts the annual cash flows each year at 25 percent and obtains a net present value of $5,575. Since the net present value is positive, Jones knows that the discount rate for the project is higher than 25 percent.

He then discounts the net cash flows at 30 percent. (The worksheet in Figure 24 does not include the annual 30 percent discount factors but they can be obtained from published tables.) The net present value at

Project: New control system

Project No.: __X7-1__

Budget amount: $40,000

| | Income/(Expenses) | | | | | | Cash (Outflow)/Inflow | | | |
Year	Sales	Manufacturing Costs	Other Costs	Depreciation for Tax Purposes	Income Tax	Profit After Tax	Depreciation for Tax Purposes	Equipment Facilities	Working Capital	Net Cash Flow
0	$ —	$ —	$(25,000)*	$ —	$12,500	$(12,500)	$ —	$(40,000)	$(50,000)	$(102,500)
1	300,000	(240,000)	(35,000)**	(13,333)	(5,834)	5,833	13,333	—	(100,000)	(80,834)
2	600,000	(480,000)	—	(10,667)	(54,666)	54,666	10,667	—	(50,000)	15,333
3	750,000	(600,000)	—	(8,000)	(71,000)	71,000	8,000	—	—	79,000
4	750,000	(600,000)	—	(5,333)	(72,333)	72,334	5,333	—	—	77,667
5	750,000	(600,000)	—	(2,667)	(73,667)	73,667	2,667	***	200,000	276,334
Totals	$3,150,000	$(2,520,000)	$(70,000)	$(40,000)	$(265,000)	$265,000	$40,000	$(40,000)	$ —	$265,000

DCF rate of return: __26.2%__

Sensitivity analysis: __-5% price__ __18.6%__

__-10% volume__ __23.2%__

* Research and development
** Promotion
*** No residual value assumed. Residual value (net of tax, if any) is shown as cash inflow at end of project.

Figure 24. Cash flow profile

30 percent is a negative $18,122. The discount rate for the project is lower than 30 percent. Through interpolation (see formula on page 81), he calculates the DCF rate for the project at 26.2 percent.

Noxton's cost of capital rate is 11.25 percent. But Jones adds 5.00 percent for the additional risks associated with introducing new products, making the acceptable rate 16.25 percent. Therefore, the new control system project DCF rate of 26.2 percent is attractive versus this standard.

However, because DCF rates of return are based on assumptions regarding price, volume, and costs, a sensitivity analysis is made. Using the same type of cash flow profile shown in Figure 24, Jones recalculates the annual cash flows assuming a 5 percent reduction in unit price from $15,000 to $14,250. The DCF rate with that assumption for the project drops from 26.2 to 18.6 percent. He also recalculates the annual cash flows assuming a 10 percent decrease in expected sales volume. The DCF rate is 23.2 percent based on the lower volume assumption.

This shows Jones that the project is relatively sensitive to the price assumption for the product. The minimum price to meet the cost of capital standard of 16.25 percent is approximately $14,000. Management's decision whether to approve the project will be based on whether it firmly believes that at least a $14,000 unit price can be obtained.

COMPARISON OF CAPITAL EXPENDITURES

Projects X7-2 and X7-3 involve buying vacuum forming machinery. However, two models of the machine are available. Model X machines cost $90,000. They will increase capacity by 15 percent. Model Y machines cost $67,500 and will increase capacity by 10 percent. Because of floor space limitations, the larger Model X machines require additional materials handling costs. Which of the two models should Noxton purchase?

The decision involves a cash outflow (for the equipment) and a series of inflows (from sales increases) that differ by model. Jones calculates the cash flows for the Model X and Model Y machines following the procedure shown in Figure 24 and summarizes them. He calculates the DCF for each model and also the DCF for the *additional* investment of $22,500 for Model X. This is shown in the column X − Y in the table below:

NET CASH FLOWS—(OUTFLOW)/INFLOW

Period	Model X	Model Y	X − Y
0	$(90,000)	$(67,500)	$(22,500)
1	47,250	41,850	5,400
2	38,250	31,050	7,200
3	29,250	20,250	9,000
4	20,250	9,450	10,800
DCF rates of return	21.8%	25.1%	14.6%

Both Model X and Model Y machines have DCF rates of return greater than Noxton's standard of 16.25 percent. But Noxton should not automatically choose the model with the higher rate of return.

The question to be asked is whether the *additional* investment in Model X of $22,500 is worthwhile to Noxton. As the table shows, the *additional* investment produces a DCF rate of return of only 14.6 percent, which is lower than Noxton's standard of 16.25 percent. Therefore, Model Y is preferable. If Noxton's cost of capital standard were lower than 14.6 percent, however, Model X would be preferable to Model Y, providing Noxton had the $22,500 to invest and no better investment opportunity was available.

PRESENT VALUE PROFILE ANALYSIS

The analysis of Model X and Model Y involves only two options. At times there may be four, five, or more choices. Calculating the incremental DCF rates of return for multiple options is cumbersome. Therefore, the present value profile helps managers when they want to choose among multiple options or test a number of assumptions for each option.

A present value profile is prepared by discounting the cash flows at various interest rates as shown in the table. The net present values are plotted on the chart shown in Figure 25. While Jones only had two options, Model X and Model Y, we have included two other model options to illustrate the principle. The net present values for Model Y are shown below:

CASH (OUTFLOW)/INFLOW—MODEL Y

Period	0%	5%	10%	15%	20%	25%
0	$(67,500)	$(67,500)	$(67,500)	$(67,500)	$(67,500)	$(67,500)
1	41,850	39,857	38,042	36,410	34,861	33,480
2	31,050	28,163	25,547	23,474	21,549	19,872
3	20,250	17,493	15,208	13,325	11,725	10,368
4	9,450	7,775	6,454	5,405	4,555	3,975
Net present value	$ 35,100	$ 25,788	$ 17,851	$ 11,114	$ 5,190	$ 95

At a 0 percent discount rate, the cash flows are the same as appear for Model Y on page 97. The net present value of the cash flows for Model Y is $35,100, which is plotted on the vertical axis of the chart at 0 percent. The net present value at 5 percent is $25,788, which is plotted at the 5 percent rate. The DCF rate of return for Model Y is 25.1 percent (see page 97) and discounting at 25 percent gives a net cash flow of only $95. The resulting curve will cross the horizontal axis at the DCF rate of return of 25.1 percent as shown. The curves for Model X and Model Y intersect at 14.6 percent, which is the incremental DCF rate of return, the calculation of which was explained on page 97. Considering only the economics of the four options plotted, the option with the *highest* net present value at Noxton's standard of 16.25 percent is preferable (Model Y).

If differences in the DCF rates of return are not large, managers may select an option which has a lower rate of return but less risk. The curves of Model W and Model Y, for example, are very close. Both have DCF rates above Noxton's standard of 16.25 percent. Either might be chosen. However, Model Y has greater cash inflow sooner than Model

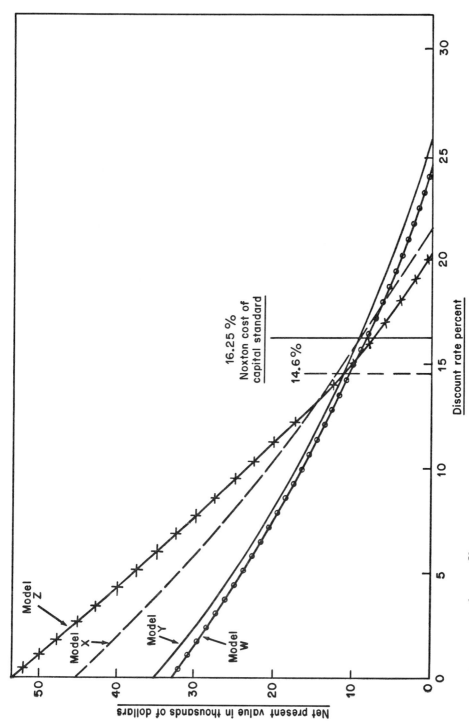

Figure 25. Present value profile

W and therefore less perceived risk. The later the cash inflow, the more risk there is that it may not be received.

PRESENT VALUE—COST COMPARISONS

In some instances, choices will need to be made between cash outflows over time without a net cash inflow. The correct decision is to select the alternative that has the *minimum* negative present value. The following table illustrates how to choose between replacing a machine or repairing a machine. The difference between the cash outflows after tax for the two alternatives gives the incremental cash flow. It is the DCF rate of return of the incremental cash flow that should be compared to the company's cost of capital standard.

AFTER-TAX CASH FLOW ANALYSIS

Year	Replace Machine	Repair Machine	Incremental Cash Flow if Replacement	Discounted at 16.25%
0	$(6,000)	$(900)	$(5,100)	$(5,100)
1	(1,250)	(2,450)	1,200	1,032
2	(1,500)	(3,200)	1,700	1,258
3	(2,000)	(3,700)	1,700	1,082
4	(1,500)	(3,950)	2,450	1,342
DCF rate of return			12.8%	$(386)

The DCF rate of return of 12.8 percent is *below* Noxton's 16.25 percent cost of capital standard. The net present value of the incremental cash flows discounted at 16.25 percent is negative by $386. Therefore, it is more economical to repair the equipment even though *total* costs over the period exceed the costs of replacing the equipment.

Net present value comparisons can also be charted as shown in Figure 26 using different discount rates. But the net present values are negative rather than positive as shown in Figure 26. The choice with the *lowest* negative present value cost at Noxton's standard rate of 16.25

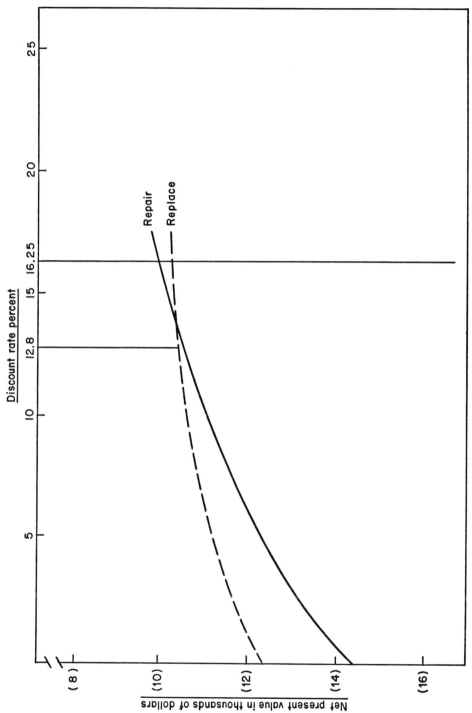

Figure 26. Present value profile—cost comparisons

percent is the best choice. The curves intersect at 12.8 percent, the incremental DCF rate of return for replacing the machine rather than repairing it as shown in the table above.

CALCULATING DISCOUNTED CASH FLOW RATE OF RETURN FOR REPLACING OLDER MACHINES

Noxton has budgeted $100,000 for four new machines. They will reduce labor and materials costs and have a life of eight years.

The machines presently in use are five years old. Maintenance and repair costs are increasing. Management believes the old machines can be used for eight more years but that maintenance and repair costs will be excessive. The new machines will also incur maintenance and repair costs after four years of use.

Jones lists the cash flows assuming an old machine is retained, and the cash flows on a new machine over the eight-year period as shown in Figure 27. In year 1 the tax depreciation of $1,667 on the old machine less maintenance and repairs produces a cash inflow of $667 before tax. The new machine, through tax depreciation, labor and materials savings produces a cash inflow of $11,667. Therefore, buying a new machine would result in an additional cash inflow in year 1 of $11,000 before tax. Assuming a 50 percent tax rate, the after-tax cash flow is $5,500. Depreciation generates cash by reducing income taxes paid. Jones will discount the *after-tax flows* to determine the DCF rate of return from investing in new machines.

The old machines can be sold for $7,265 each. Their value for tax purposes (tax basis) has been reduced by depreciation deductions to $3,335. Therefore, Noxton will incur a tax on $3,930 ($7,265 − $3,335 = $3,930 × 50% tax rate) in the amount of $1,965. The selling price of $7,265 less the tax is $5,300. This amount can be used to reduce the cash investment in a new machine for evaluation purposes.

Each new machine costs $25,000 plus installation charges of $1,500 for a total cost of $26,500. The $26,500 can be reduced by $5,300 that would be realized from sale of an old machine for a net cash investment in year 0 of $21,200 to determine the DCF rate of return. The rate that discounts the annual cash flow differences after tax shown in Figure 27 to $21,200 is 19 percent. Because 19 percent exceeds Noxton's cost of

Cash (outflow)/inflow   Net cash investment (year 0): $(21,200)

	Old Machine			New Machine					
Year	Depreciation for Tax Purposes	Maintenance and Repairs	Total Cash Flow	Depreciation for Tax Purposes	Maintenance and Repairs	Labor and Materials Savings	Total Cash Flow	Total Cash Flow Difference	Cash Flow Difference After Tax
1	$1,667	$(1,000)	$ 667	$ 5,889	$ —	$ 5,778	$11,667	$11,000	$ 5,500
2	1,111	(1,000)	111	5,153	—	5,958	11,111	11,000	5,500
3	557	(1,000)	(443)	4,417	—	6,140	10,557	11,000	5,500
4	—	(2,000)	(2,000)	3,681	(2,000)	6,719	8,400	10,400	5,200
5	—	(2,000)	(2,000)	2,944	(1,500)	6,956	8,400	10,400	5,200
6	—	(2,000)	(2,000)	2,208	(1,000)	7,192	8,400	10,400	5,200
7	—	(2,000)	(2,000)	1,472	(1,000)	7,928	8,400	10,400	5,200
8	—	(2,000)	(2,000)	736	(1,000)	8,664	8,400	10,400	5,200
Total	$3,335	$(13,000)	$(9,665)	$26,500	$(6,500)	$55,335	$75,335	$85,000	$42,500

Figure 27. Development of cash flows—new machines vs. old machines

capital standard rate of 16.25 percent, buying the new machines is an attractive investment opportunity for Noxton.

CALCULATING DCF RATE OF RETURN ON A WAREHOUSE INVESTMENT

Noxton currently rents a considerable amount of commercial warehouse space. The budget includes a proposal for Noxton to build a warehouse adjacent to the plant at a cost of $105,000. The warehouse would save Noxton about $33,500 per year in storage and handling charges. The estimated life of the warehouse is 20 years. At a 50 percent tax rate, the after-tax savings from having the warehouse are $16,750. The rate that discounts 20, annual cash inflows of $16,750 to $105,000 is about 15 percent, which is slightly less than Noxton's cost of capital standard.

Although the DCF rate of return for the warehouse investment is below the cost of capital standard of 16.25 percent for new projects, it is still above Noxton's cost of capital of 11.25 percent by a good margin. Because the risk of not achieving the cost savings is low with this type of investment, management may decide to build its own warehouse.

CAPITAL INVESTMENTS THAT REQUIRE SPECIAL HANDLING

In most projects, cash flows will consist of an investment outflow followed by a series of inflows or outflows. However, with some types of projects, cash flows do not follow that pattern. Instead, there are cash outflows followed by inflows and followed by outflows again. If there is a significant change in the pattern of cash flow over the life of the project, it is possible that two or more DCF rates of return can be obtained.

The easiest solution for handling such projects is to plot them on a present value profile similar to that shown in Figure 26. The curve may cross the horizontal axis at two different points. Therefore, the projects cannot be described in terms of a single DCF rate of return. Instead, they have to be evaluated by reference to their present value at the minimum acceptable rate of return standard. For example, the following project has a significant change in its cash flow pattern:

Year	Cash Flows
0	$(10,000)
1	60,000
2	(110,000)
3	60,000

There is a significant reversal in cash flow in years 2 and 3 since the cumulative net cash flows go from a positive to a negative and back to zero. There are three interest rates that will discount these cash flows to zero. They are 0 percent, 100 percent and 200 percent. At Noxton's 16.25 percent standard, however, the present value of the cash flows is negative by $1,400. Projects which have a positive present value at 16.25 percent would take precedence over this project.

RANKING PROJECTS BY DCF RATES OF RETURN

Jones can rank Noxton budget proposals by their DCF rates of return which are as follows:

	Amount	DCF
New control system	$ 40,000	26.2%
Vacuum forming	67,500*	25.1*
Four new machines	100,000	19.0
Warehouse	105,000	15.0
Other	62,500	—
Total	$375,000	—

*The $67,500 and 25.1 percent are based on purchasing Model Y.

Noxton's management can now allocate available funds for capital investment in the order of the investment projects' profit contributions. If capital is extremely short, perhaps funds for only one or two projects will be authorized. It appears from the above list, however, that Noxton can profitably invest about $375,000 of capital in 19X7, depending on the decision for the warehouse, and management should take reasonable measures to ensure the capital is available for these investments.

VII

How Financial Planning Contributes to Reaching Profit Goals

Financial planning starts with setting long-term goals. In this case study, Noxton's long-term goals include an increase of sales to $22 million in five years, and improvement of earnings per share by at least 10 percent per year.

Noxton does not set fixed return on investment goals. Instead, senior management, with assistance from the operating managers, sets net profit objectives each year using updated cost of capital standards. The cost of capital standard is the minimum acceptable result and Noxton attempts to exceed it.

Long-term goals reflect management's strategies regarding market share, products, production techniques, manufacturing capacity, and profitability. They are supported by short-term objectives which focus on sales, costs, and profits for the current year. Managers develop detailed plans to achieve these short-term objectives.

SHORT-TERM PLANNING

Noxton's operating managers were asked in late 19X6 to submit forecasts for 19X7, 19X8 and 19X9. The company prepares a forecast each year for the following three years. After senior management review and approval, the first year of the forecast becomes the company's operating and financial plan. Noxton's operating and financial plan includes detailed budgets covering sales, production, number of employees, labor efficiency, material purchases and usage, departmental expenses, and so on. Management compares actual results to budgets each month during the year. Significant variations from budget are investigated, and corrective actions are taken where necessary.

THE SALES FORECAST

The sales department estimates sales units by product for 19X7, 19X8 and 19X9. The total 19X7 unit sales exceed units sold in 19X6 by 6.5 percent. Next, all product prices are reviewed relative to those of competitors and Noxton's own cost estimates for 19X7.

For example, Noxton estimates that labor costs will increase by 4.5 percent in 19X7 and material costs will increase 7.0 percent. Special attention is given to pricing products that earned less than the cost of capital standard in 19X6, as was shown in the circuit breaker analysis in Section V. Jones prepares worksheets for pricing products in 19X7 using the asset and cost allocation procedures described in Section V. His worksheet for circuit breakers is shown in Figure 28. The 19X7 costs are estimated, and the 19X6 actual results are included for reference purposes.

Figure 28 shows that estimated 19X7 unit sales for circuit breakers are 15,950, a 10 percent increase over 19X6. The 19X7 cost of capital profit goal for circuit breakers is estimated at $335,000 or $21.00 per unit based on sales of 15,950 units. Management believes it can increase circuit breaker prices without affecting the estimated sales volume. Therefore, the 19X7 price that produces a unit profit of $21.00 is $183.45, a 10.8 percent unit price increase over 19X6. Noxton's senior management agrees to this new price.

No changes in the product are planned that would change the

CIRCUIT BREAKERS

	Forecast 19X7			Actual 19X6			Change 19X7 vs. 19X6	
	15,950			14,500				
	Units	%	Total	Units	%	Total	Units	$ Totals
Sales units							+10.0%	—
Sales	$183.45	100.0	$2,920	$165.50	100.0	$2,405	+ 10.8%	+ 21.4%
Cost of sales								
Direct labor	27.69	15.1	442	26.50	16.0	385	+ 4.5%	+ 14.8%
Materials	74.38	40.5	1,186	69.51	42.0	1,010	+ 7.0%	+ 17.4%
Overhead & other	43.13	23.5	688	45.06	27.3	655	– 4.3%	+ 5.0%
Gross margin	$ 38.25	20.9	$ 610	$ 24.43	14.8	$ 345	+ 56.6%	+ 76.8%
Selling, adminis-trative, and other costs	17.25	9.4	275	17.67	10.7	257	– 2.4%	+ 7.0%
Profit before tax	$ 21.00	11.4	$ 335	$ 6.76	4.1	$ 98	+310.7%	+341.8%
Cost of capital goal	$ 21.00		$ 335	$ 21.04		$ 324	– 0.2%	+ 3.4%
Residual income before tax	—		—	$(14.28)		$(226)	N.A.	N.A.

Note: 000 omitted

Figure 28. Worksheet for pricing products

direct labor or material costs per unit in 19X7. However, because of expected cost increases, the estimated 19X7 unit costs for direct labor and materials are increased from the 19X6 actual amount per unit by 4.5 and 7.0 percent, respectively. No offsetting labor efficiency improvements are expected. Overhead and other costs are then applied on the basis of allocations obtained from the controller.

While the above forecast applies to circuit breakers, competitive factors prohibit the prices of some other products in the industrial products line to be increased at all in 19X7. Other product prices are increased but their unit sales are reduced.

Management's objective in pricing is to maximize the residual income or contribution to the cost of capital profit goal for each product. After a complete review of each product, using the same method as described for circuit breakers, Noxton decides that an increase of its unit prices by an average for all products of 7.5 percent over 19X6 can be achieved. The total 19X7 dollar sales objective is therefore fixed at $16.5 million, 14.5 percent above 19X6.

PREPARATION OF COST ESTIMATES

Department managers make preliminary estimates of their costs and review them with senior management. An initial review allows management to assess cost trends after knowing the estimated sales volume and to make adjustments that consider the long-term goals and the short-term outlook.

After the review, the sales forecast and the departmental costs for each product are consolidated by Noxton's treasurer to obtain total company forecasts. The consolidation results in a preliminary net income estimate of $650,000 for 19X7, 13 percent above 19X6 results of $575,000.

COMPARISON OF ESTIMATES WITH COST OF CAPITAL STANDARDS

To test the adequacy of preliminary estimates, Jones calculates net income for 19X7 based on Noxton's minimum cost of capital standard of 11.25 percent as shown in the following table. The interest adjustment of $123,500 is calculated by multiplying $2,500,000 by 9.5 percent and multiplying the result by 1.00 minus the effective tax rate of 48 percent in this example.

Total capital beginning 19X7	$7,980,000
Capital multiplied by .1125	$ 897,750
Less: Interest on long-term debt of $2,500,000 at cost of capital rate. (9.5% interest cost net of income tax savings)	123,500
Cost of capital net income goal for 19X7	$ 774,250

The minimum cost of capital net income goal of $774,250 exceeds Noxton's preliminary forecast of $650,000 by $124,250. Even though Noxton has not had earnings equal to its cost of capital standard in recent years, management believes that income can be increased to the standard in 19X7 if tougher cost objectives are set by department managers. Price and volume increases beyond those estimated are not possible. To achieve the standard income, therefore, the preliminary cost estimates must be reduced by $239,000 before tax ($124,250 ÷ [1.00 − .48 tax rate] = $239,000).

Cost estimates are reviewed again with department managers. Selling and administration expenses are cut by 6 percent, and labor, material, and manufacturing overhead costs are cut $153,000 or 1.1 percent. The 19X7 total cost of sales estimate comes to $13,377,000, representing 81.1 percent of the $16,500,000 sales estimate. This compares to an actual cost of sales in 19X6 of $11,775,000 and 81.7 percent.

All Noxton managers have set much tougher cost objectives for 19X7. These tougher goals are the direct result of using cost of capital as an analytical tool. Higher sales in 19X7 with controlled costs result in a significant improvement to 10.3 percent in Noxton's operating margin. This reverses the declining trend since 19X4 that was shown in Section III, page 36, in the operating ratios.

ANALYSIS OF PROJECTED CASH FLOW

As shown in Figure 29, the treasurer has prepared a projected income statement and balance sheet for 19X7. Before the consolidation took

STATEMENT OF INCOME
(000 omitted)

	Projected 19X7	Actual 19X6	19X7 vs. 19X6 % Change
Sales	$16,500	$14,415	+14.5
Cost of sales	13,377	11,775	+13.6
Selling and shipping expenses	780	725	+ 7.6
Administrative and general expense	640	600	+ 6.7
Operating income	1,703	1,315	+29.5
Interest and other income	35	35	—
Interest and other expense	(250)	(250)	—
Income before tax	1,488	1,100	+35.3
Income tax	714	525	+36.0
Net income	$ 774	$ 575	+34.6

BALANCE SHEET

	Projected 19X7	Actual 19X6		Projected 19X7	Actual 19X6
Cash	$ 698	$ 890	Accounts payable	$ 1,360	$ 1,160
Accounts receivable	1,672	1,472	Notes payable	—	600
Inventory	4,500	4,300	Income tax payable	324	100
Prepaid expense	40	40			
Total current assets	6,910	6,702	Other payable	470	430
			Total current liabilities	2,154	2,290
Land	450	450			
Buildings	2,605	2,500	Long-term debt	2,500	2,500
Machinery and equipment	2,645	2,400	Deferred income tax	300	300
Total	5,700	5,350			

Figure 29. Projected income statement and balance sheet

BALANCE SHEET *continued*

	Projected 19X7	Actual 19X6		Projected 19X7	Actual 19X6
Reserve for depreciation	(1,897)	(1,557)	Stockholders' equity	5,834	5,480
Net long-term assets	3,803	3,793	Total liabilities		
Other assets	75	75	and equity		
Total assets	$10,788	$10,570		$10,788	$10,570

Figure 29. Continued

place, each departmental projection was subjected to the same kind of review, analysis, testing projected results against cost of capital standards and adjustments as was illustrated by the circuit breaker example earlier in this Section.

Figure 30 shows the cash flow statement, the financing, and the free cash flow. The cash flow statement reveals an estimated cash generation in 19X7 of $408,000. This compares to a cash shortage of $110,000 in 19X6.

The $408,000, with an additional $192,000 cash on hand, will be used in 19X7 to repay the $600,000 short-term working capital loan which was outstanding at the end of 19X6.

The cash flow statement shows capital expenditures in 19X7 of $350,000. This estimate covers all the approved budget projects listed on page 93. The statement also anticipates that the warehouse project will be approved, but that of the $105,000 budget amount, $25,000 will not be spent until 19X8.

Of the total capital expenditures forecast for 19X7, $207,500 is for various machinery which can be leased. In Section IV, Jones computed Noxton's leasing capability in 19X7 at $235,000.

However, Jones believes that Noxton's cash flow in 19X7 will be adequate for dividends, short-term note repayments, capital expenditures, and other requirements, so that leasing will not be necessary. Leasing will be an alternative for Noxton, however, should cash flow fall below planned levels.

CASH FLOW STATEMENT
(000 omitted)

	Projected 19X7	Actual 19X6
Source of cash		
Net profit before tax	$1,488	$1,100
Depreciation	340	325
Total	1,828	1,425
Uses of cash		
Capital expenditures	350	200
Increase in current accounts	160	540
Taxes paid	490	445
Long-term debt repaid	—	—
Dividends paid	420	350
Total	1,420	1,535
Cash long/(short)	408	(110)
Financing		
Short-term notes increase/(decrease)	(600)	100
New long-term debt	—	—
Cash (increase)/decrease	192	10

FREE CASH FLOW

	Projected 19X7	Actual 19X6
Dividends paid	$ 420	$ 350
Cash increase/(decrease)	(192)	(10)
Debt decrease/(increase)	600	(100)
Interest expense net of tax	104	105
Total	$ 932	$ 345

Figure 30. Projected cash flow statement and free cash flow

It is also possible for the capital budget to be increased during the year should attractive investment opportunities arise. Jones has several options available for financing additional expenditures. He can use cash and reduce the balance temporarily, defer repayment of the short-term notes, obtain new bank credit or lease. The decision can be made at the time depending on actual circumstances.

USES OF COST OF CAPITAL PROFIT STANDARDS

As shown in Section VI, cost of capital profit standards can be used to evaluate the earning power of individual projects. For example, the major projects included in Noxton's 19X7 capital budget all exceed the *minimum* cost of capital standard of 11.25 percent by a good margin to compensate for their risk. The excess also permits expenditures for cafeteria equipment and other items that need to be made regardless of the return. Noxton's senior management is therefore assured that planned new capital investments meet investor expectations.

EVALUATION OF PRODUCT, DIVISION AND COMPANY PROFIT GOALS

Cost of capital profit standards can also be used to set division or product profit goals. Noxton does not have divisions. But Jones applied the concept to products as was described in Section V. It was also used by Noxton to help set prices and volumes for 19X7.

Cost of capital profit standards are also used for setting the total company's profit goal. Jones applied Noxton's minimum cost of capital standard of 11.25 percent to develop the company's planned net income goal in 19X7 of $774,000. This use led management to set tighter cost limits throughout the company to achieve the net income objective. In 19X8 a new cost of capital standard will be used to ensure equally demanding performance objectives.

USE OF STANDARDS TO ALLOCATE CAPITAL

Cost of capital standards are used to allocate capital among divisions or product lines to maximize the return on total investment. This is usually done in long-range strategic planning. For example, divisions or products which are highly profitable when measured by the cost of capital standard should be expanded.

New capital investment in already successful product lines will most likely produce high returns. However, in divisions or products which show only a modest return relative to cost of capital, management should concentrate on increasing volume and prices and reducing costs rather than adding new capital. In fact, the rate of return for such divisions or products may actually improve if capital is reduced and new capital invested only when necessary to continue production.

Divisions or products which continually show an unsatisfactory rate of return after taking all reasonable measures should receive no new capital. The correct decision in most of these cases will be to discontinue the operation and free what capital remains for use elsewhere in the company.

USE OF RETURN ON ASSETS RATES

The cost of capital concept can therefore be constructively used to decide *where* capital should be invested as well as the return to be expected. Figure 31 shows how this concept applies to a number of divisions or products for a four-year period. In this example, assets are used as the base because they can be allocated more easily than capital. However, the concept of return on assets is equivalent to the cost of capital concept and provides useful standards for measurement. At times, some assets such as excess cash reserves cannot be allocated to specific divisions or products and a line is provided on the schedule for such assets.

The total rate of return on assets of 8.3 percent in 19X7 as shown in Figure 31 has been calculated as follows:

Forecast net income		$ 774,000
Actual interest expense net of income tax savings		104,000
Adjusted net income	(A)	$ 878,000
Total assets beginning of year	(B)	$10,570,000
Return on assets	(A) ÷ (B)	8.3%

FORECAST
(000 omitted)

Division or Product	19X7		19X8		19X9		19X0	
	Assets	Return on Assets	Assets	Return on Assets	Assets	Return on Assets	Assets	Return on Assets
A	$ 4,250	10.3%	$ 4,400	11.0%	$ 4,700	11.6%	$ 5,100	12.0%
B	1,400	8.6	1,550	9.0	1,650	10.4	1,850	10.8
C	2,500	8.3	2,550	8.5	2,630	8.5	2,700	8.8
D	750*	8.2*	700*	8.0*	700*	7.8*	650	8.5
E	1,400*	7.0*	1,375*	8.0*	1,355	8.5	1,300	9.0
F	270*	negative*	213*	negative*	185*	6.5*	—	—
G (new product)	—	—	—	—	—	—	—	—
Unallocated	—	—	—	—	—	—	180	8.3
Total	$10,570	8.3%	$10,788	9.3%	$11,220	10.0%	$11,780	10.5%

*Does not meet minimum return on assets standard of 8.3%.

Figure 31. Estimated return on assets by product—19X7 to 19X0

The 8.3 percent and other rates of return on assets shown in the schedule in Figure 31 are net *after* income tax. They assume no interest expense in order to facilitate cost allocations. However, *before* tax rates can also be used if tax allocations to products or divisions would distort results.

The total rate of return on assets increases from 8.3 percent in 19X7 to 10.5 percent in 19X0 reflecting estimated income growth above the return on assets standard of 8.3 percent. The higher rates of return are achieved largely by investing new capital in the more profitable A and B products.

INTERPRETATION OF RETURN ON ASSETS RATES

By examining the assets invested in each product and the rate of return on assets over the four-year period, it becomes clear that the rate of return on one product cannot be compared directly to another. Also, managers cannot expect to achieve continued increases in the rate of return on every product. The importance to managers is to learn what rate of return can reasonably be expected in light of the investment, competitive situation, and where the product is in its growth cycle.

For example, products A and B are very profitable in relation to the minimum cost of capital standard (equivalent to an 8.3 percent return on assets standard). The rates of return are expected to improve over the four-year period. New capital should be allocated to these products to maximize total profit. Product C, however, is only moderately profitable, but some improvement in the rate of return can be expected with a moderate amount of new capital investment.

Products D and E do not earn the minimum rates of return until the amount of capital invested in assets is reduced, as Figure 31 shows for later years. Therefore, new capital will not be allocated to these products. Product F is very unprofitable and the forecast plans to phase it out entirely in 19X0 in favor of a new product projected to be more profitable, product G.

Managers responsible for division or product profitability should be measured against standards for their own division or product. A manager of one division or product may earn less than another but still

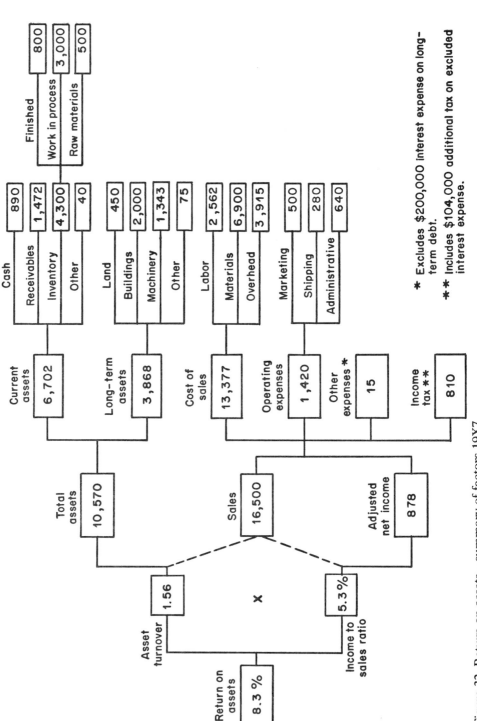

Figure 32. Return on assets—summary of factors 19X7

perform just as well. It is the standards of his own division or product that are important to the total company objective.

USES OF RETURN ON ASSETS

The 8.3 percent return on assets projected for 19X7 is the minimum acceptable rate of return based on Noxton's 11.25 percent cost of capital. The assets, sales, and costs can be allocated to divisions, products, departments, cost centers, and so forth to set goals and control progress toward achieving cost of capital standards throughout the company.

Figure 32 illustrates how the 8.3 percent return on assets relates to all the factors that are used to calculate it. The figures in the upper half of the diagram relate to assets and are taken from the balance sheet. The figures in the lower half relate to income and come from the statement of income.

The schematic approach to developing return on assets helps financial managers to determine ways to improve results. Through the diagram they can measure the effects on the return of changes from budget in sales, costs, and assets.

The ultimate objective of the financial manager is to help senior management to achieve a rate of return on assets consistently above the minimum cost of capital rate. When this is accomplished, top management can be said to be successfully managing the investors' capital.

Appendix:
The Capman Model,
A Lotus 1-2-3 Based Model
for Capital Management

Now that you have finished reading CAPITAL MANAGEMENT FOR FINANCIAL EXECUTIVES, you know the techniques that successful managers use to get maximum returns from the capital of their firms.

But there is one additional technique that is becoming more important every day: using a microcomputer to manage capital. Not only can a microcomputer keep neat, accurate records of all the numbers that it receives, but it can print them out on a moment's notice. More importantly for financial managers, financial analysts and students of financial management, a microcomputer lets you try out financial strategies on the video screen or make "for your eyes only" printouts to check before you take your strategies for review to a bank, your board of directors, or investors.

To show you how effective financial modeling can be with a microcomputer, Alexander Hamilton Institute has created a computer program called "Capman" which will work with your own IBM PC and Lotus 1-2-3.* The Capman program will build your financial management skills in two important ways:

*See copyright page for ordering information.

1. It puts you in the place of the financial manager of the Noxton Corporation, with which you are already familiar, and takes you through its financial statements. Then, you must use modeling techniques to meet the financial goals which Noxton's top management sets for you.

2. It provides you with your own financial models, all laid out neatly in columns and rows. All you need to do is enter your own company's items and figures or do a simulation of any company. You will then have a flexible, working financial model which you can print, update, alter or review at any time.

Please note that while Capman will show you certain techniques for using Lotus for financial modeling and capital management, it is *not* designed to teach you how to use Lotus 1-2-3 itself.

USING CAPMAN ON YOUR COMPUTER

Before you begin using Capman, you should *make a copy of the diskette.* Keep the original in a safe place, a clean and dry environment away from strong magnetic fields. If anything happens to the copy of the diskette as you use it, you can make another copy from the original. If you need help in copying Capman to a floppy diskette, refer to your DOS manual.

If you have a hard disk system, you will also want to copy all of the files on the Capman diskette onto the appropriate directory on your hard disk. Again, refer to your DOS manual if you need help.

DESCRIPTION OF THE FILES ON THE CAPMAN DISKETTE

There are four files on the diskette:

1. CAPMAN.WKS—This is the file with Noxton Corporation's financial statements on it. You will use it to develop a financial strategy.

2. CM.WKS—This file is a blank financial model which you

can use for managing your own company's capital, or that of a simulated or competitor company. It also provides the capability of customizing the model.

3. CMNXTN.WKS—This file contains Noxton Corporation's financial records *and* customizing capabilities. It is designed to illustrate the operations involved in customizing a model and for those who wish to experiment further with the Noxton example.

4. PRINTER.WKS—This file contains the setup codes for the printer to be used with Capman on your PC. Thus, you have the opportunity to configure your system when you load Capman.

LOADING CAPMAN

Boot up Lotus 1-2-3 on your PC. If you have a two floppy disk drive machine, place your copy of Capman in drive B. Next type /FRCAPMAN and hit the "Return" key. You will see the Capman Main Menu on the viewing screen after a brief wait.

OVERVIEW OF THE SYSTEM

The Capman system has been set up with a command menu structure using Lotus 1-2-3's so-called "macro" capabilities. Six main menu items are displayed on the third line of your screen (see the Main Menu on the screen).

Menu items are selected by either:

1. Moving to the menu item of your choice by using your PC's cursor movement keys and then hitting the "Return" key. (You will notice that a few words of description appear below the highlighted menu item on line four of your screen.)

2. Typing the first letter or number of the menu item of your choice.

Try the following example:

With the main menu on your screen [1) View, 2) Projection, 3) Print, 4) File, 5) Work, 6) Quit] move the cursor over to number 3, PRINT, by pressing the → key twice. Then press "Return." You will see the PRINT menu. You don't want to print any financial statements right now, so choose the Menu option to return to the previous menu.

Rather than spacing over to Menu to make the choice, simply type the first letter, in this case M. If a menu item has a number in front of it, type in that number rather than the first letter.

In general, choosing a menu item will result in the display of a subsequent menu allowing for a more detailed selection of options. However, choosing Menu from any menu in which that option exists will result in the display of the previously displayed menu.

There are five options on the Main Menu. Each of these and its main branches is described below.

1. View—Allows you to view a financial statement with the subsequent opportunity to do a new projection by viewing a split screen with Forecast Assumptions in the top window and the chosen statement in the bottom window. New assumptions can be entered and the resulting changes will appear in the financial statements.

After the screen is split, Lotus 1-2-3's mode indicator (upper right corner of screen) will read CMD READY with the cursor resting on the first assumption. You may use the up or down cursor movement keys to move to the appropriate cell to enter a new assumption. If you have entered a number in the column containing the Forecast Assumptions, you must hit the "Return" key two successive times for the system to accept your entry and recalculate the values in the various financial statements. If you have chosen to make a projection but, before entering any values, decide that you would rather not make any changes in Forecast Assumptions, simply hit the "Return" key once. The system will recalculate all formulas, but no statement numbers will change as no assumption was changed.

Try the following example:

Choose the View option from the Main Menu. Then choose option 3 from the next menu, the Cash Flow Statement. The system will display the Cash Flow Statement and menu choices, Projection and Menu. Type P for Projection. You will then see a split screen of Forecast Assumptions and the bottom half of the Cash Flow Statement. You may scroll up or down in the bottom window by choosing numbers 2 and 3, respectively, from this menu.

Now, type a 1 for Enter Projection Figures. Using the down arrow cursor movement key, move the cursor to the Accounts Receivable line which is currently set at 10% of Sales (Coordinate D106). Type in a 9 and hit "Return" twice. After a few seconds, you will see the figures in the Cash Flow Statement change. Then type 1 again, and move the cursor back down to Accounts Receivable. Enter a 10 and hit the "Return" key twice to restore the original values. Then type M three times to move back up the menu structure until you are back at the Main Menu.

2. Projection—While the View option allows you to make projections by giving you five lines of Forecast Assumptions in one window and 14 lines of a selected financial statement in a second window, the Projection option from the Main Menu displays *all* of the Forecast Assumptions on the screen at once and then permits you to enter new assumptions. You may then see the resulting changes in a financial statement by selecting the View option from the Main Menu and choosing the financial statement you want to review.

3. Print—Allows you to print the Forecast Assumptions, any financial statement, or the Forccast Assumptions and *all* the financial statements and configure your system for printer type.

4. File—The File option on the Main Menu has three branches:

- Save. Saves the current Capman worksheet to disk.
- Backup. Backups current Capman to disk with file name of your choice. Upon completion of Backup, system will put you in READY mode. *In order to reenter the Capman menu structure, you must type the Alt and M keys simultaneously.*
- Retrieve. Permits you to retrieve another worksheet without leaving the Capman menu structure. You might use this when switching between the Noxton model and your customized model.

There is also a Menu choice to return you to the previous menu.

5. Work—Gets you out of the Capman command menu structure putting you in READY model and thus allows you to move freely around the spreadsheet to inspect formulas and cell contents. With the Mode Indicator reading "Ready," to get back into the Capman menu system

press the Alt and M keys simultaneously. WARNING: *Never hit Alt and M together unless the Mode Indicator reads "Ready."* Note that there is a Work option on the View menu as well.

      6. Quit—Choosing the Quit option takes you from 1-2-3 and returns to the Lotus Access System.

CONFIGURING YOUR SYSTEM FOR PRINTER TYPE

While viewing the Main Menu, type 3 for Print. You will then see a menu with the choices 1) Print Statements, 2) Configure System, and Menu. Choose number 2. You will see a menu with four dot matrix printers represented: EPSON/IBM, C.ITOH, and OKIDATA. If you have one of these, select the appropriate choice. The relevant setup string will then be saved to PRINTER.WKS to be read in later when you instruct the system to print out Forecast Assumptions and/or the financial statements.

      If you have a letter-quality printer, select option 5 from this menu. When printing from Capman configured for a letter-quality printer, no control codes will be sent. The system will assume that one font will be used and 132 columns of text will be printed across a page. The system will save this configuration to disk.

      If you have a printer not represented on the Printer Type Menu, select option 6, Other. Check your printer manual to determine the exact setup code your printer requires to print in *condensed type*. When you enter this code in response to the LOTUS prompt "Enter Setup String," make sure that these ASCII codes have been properly translated into LOTUS \nnn format as outlined in the Lotus 1-2-3 Manual. When this code is entered it will be saved to PRINTER.WKS.

      You only need to configure your system for your printer type one time unless you change printers.

REVIEWING THE SYSTEM

      1. Menu items are selected either by spacing over to the desired option and then pressing "Return," or typing the first number or letter of the menu choice.

2. When in any menu other than the Main Menu, you may return to the previous menu by selecting the Menu option.

3. When you have chosen to make a new projection, whether from View or Projection in the Main Menu, and the Mode Indicator reads CMD READY, use the cursor movement keys to move into the appropriate cell to enter the new assumption. Hitting the "Return" key twice in succession will enter new assumptions and permit the system to recalculate the values in the financial statements. If you are in the CMD READY mode and hit the "Return" key without entering a number, the system will retain all present values and return you to the menu.

4. If you have chosen the Work menu option, which allows you to move freely around the sheet with the Mode Indicator reading "Ready," you can get back into the Capman menu system by pressing the Alt and M keys simultaneously. WARNING: *Never hit Alt and M together unless the Mode Indicator reads "Ready."*

5. Make sure that you have configured the program for your printer by choosing Print from the Main Menu and then the appropriate Configure option.

GETTING TO KNOW THE FINANCIAL STATEMENTS

You are now ready to review Noxton's financial statements on your screen. You should currently be viewing Noxton's major Forecast Assumptions which were listed previously. If you are not looking at this information, hit M to return to the previous menu until you see the Main Menu. Then type 2 for Projection and 1 for Enter Assumptions. Then hit the "Return" key. All of the assumptions relate to sales except for the capital expenditures assumption. They are all based on Noxton's experience in recent years.

This model assumes that annual capital expenditures for the three forecast years, 19X7, 19X8 and 19X9, will be higher than recent years because of a higher growth in sales. Jones has used a 10 percent annual investment rate which assumes that Noxton's fixed assets have an average life of about 10 years. (An 8 percent investment rate would assume an average life of 12.5 years.) The 10 percent rate is the lowest investment rate for Noxton to ensure that production capacity is sufficient in all forecast years to support the sales growth objective.

When you are finished reviewing the assumptions, type 1 to see Capman's View Menu. What follows is a "guided tour" of Noxton's finances. Now type the number 1 twice. Noxton's actual statements of income for 19X6 and 19X5 now appear on the screen. Now type the number 2. The screen should show the forecast income statements for 19X7, 19X8, and 19X9.

You will note that the ratios of all the costs to the annual sales values, except for the interest expenses, do not change from year to year. But the interest expense is increasing and the net income is decreasing relative to sales. This is the result of additional borrowings during the forecast period at an interest rate assumed to be 10 percent.

When you have finished viewing the income statements, type M to return to the previous menu. Now type the number 2 to see Information for Cash Flow.

This schedule summarizes the net change each year in the current accounts, which will appear in the annual cash flow statements. It also makes some additional assumptions for annual depreciation, other payables and taxes paid. You can review these assumptions, which are necessary to complete the cash flow statements. One easy way to see the assumptions is to return to the previous menu and then type the number 6 for Work so that you can move the cursor through the cells, one by one, and see the formulas displayed there.

For example, if you look at F162, Other Payables for 19X7, you will see the formula .03*(I131 + I134 + I135). This tells you that Other Payables for 19X7 total 3 percent of the sum of the cost of sales, plus selling expenses, plus administrative expense, for 19X7.

To return to the Capman menu structure, type the Alt and M keys simultaneously. Return to the View menu by typing the number 1 and then choose number 3 to see the forecast cash flow statements, which show Noxton's yearly financing requirements based on all the assumptions. This is a very important part of Noxton's forecast, since negative cash flows indicate a need for new financing. In fact, the annual new financing requirements are $582,000 for 19X7, $675,000 for 19X8, and $767,000 for 19X9. Meeting these requirements for funds while staying within the guidelines of Noxton's management is the most important part of your job.

Now type M to return to the View menu and type 4 and then 1

to see the assets side of the balance sheet. Note the annual growth in accounts receivable and inventories, while plant and equipment grows to a sizable sum too.

By typing the number 2 from the displayed menu, you can review the forecast of liabilities and net worth. Notice that the growth of new financing necessary by the end of 19X9 is about double the growth of shareholders' equity. Debt caused by new financing will be $2,024,000, while shareholders' equity increases by only $1,016,000. This affects Noxton's long-term debt to equity ratio and may affect its credit rating in a manner that is inconsistent with management's objectives.

Now hit M to return to the View menu and then type the number 5 to see a summary of the key items from all statements plus four important ratios, including the long-term debt to equity ratio. Note the substantial increase in the total liabilities to equity and long-term debt to equity ratios. However, there is an increase in the rate of return on equity. Some of this increase is caused by the increased leverage that comes from the growing debt ratio. Therefore, the higher return on equity is reflecting a higher risk in addition to an improved operating performance.

The rate of return on capital also increases and, as discussed in the text of CAPITAL MANAGEMENT, it eliminates the interest cost effect of long-term debt. This rate can be compared to the firm's weighted average cost of capital.

TAKING CHARGE OF NOXTON'S FINANCES

Now you must take the finances in your own hands. Using Lotus 1-2-3, you can try a number of different strategies to find the best one to meet top management's objectives.

From your reading of the text of this book, you know that Noxton's sales have been growing at about an 8 percent compound rate in recent years and that its capital structure is relatively conservative.

However, management has now set an objective of an 18 percent sales growth per year. That will require more capital investment in assets such as inventory, accounts receivable, plant and equipment. You must assess the impact of this growth rate on the financial structure of the company for the next three years. The sales growth will cause increases in cost of sales, other costs and capital expenditures. The Forecast Assumptions show the relationships. For instance, the cost of sales is 81.5 percent of sales in Noxton's model.

You must also calculate the financing requirement—how much additional money Noxton will need—and recommend where the money should come from so that Noxton's credit, financial structure, and other guidelines set out by management are met.

You know that funds to finance asset growth can come from only three sources:

1. Retaining more profits (lower dividend payout).
2. Increasing liabilities (more debt).
3. Selling new equity stock.

The sale of stock is not used in Noxton's model, but you can include it in your own customized model.

Noxton's top management has given you the following objectives and guidelines for the coming three years:

1. Sales growth of 18 percent per year.
2. No lowering of firm's credit rating.
3. No significant increase in financial risk by incurring a large amount of additional debt.
4. Maintain a 60 percent dividend payout rate if possible, but a payout as low as 50 percent will be acceptable.
5. Reduce inventory, if necessary, to meet the objectives, but not below 33 percent of cost of sales because that would risk shortages and delivery problems.
6. The cost of sales percent of sales can be reduced, but not below 80 percent.

In other words, you can adjust (1) cost of sales, (2) inventories, and (3) dividends paid to accomplish the goals, as long as you meet the overall balance that management needs. You will do it by changing these three Assumptions at the very beginning of the statements.

Here are a few pieces of advice, in order of importance, that can guide you.

1. Select View from the Main Menu and then choose Key Lines from the next menu. Then type P for Projection. You can now scroll

through all the assumptions on the top portion of the screen, make changes as necessary, and see the resulting changes in the key ratios on the bottom portion of the screen.

2. You can change more than one assumption at a time, but you will not be able to tell which change has the largest impact on the key ratios (or on the financial statements). Therefore, initially at least, change only one assumption at a time. You should soon discover what the combination of cost of sales, inventories and dividends must be to produce acceptable total liabilities and long-term debt to equity ratios in all forecast years. You can check your answer against the one on page 140.

3. Don't hesitate to use trial and error, because the computer can do your calculations for you incredibly quickly. And if you fear you have messed up the spreadsheet, just return to the Main Menu, choose number 4, File, and then number 3, Retrieve, from the next menu. In response to the prompt "Enter name of file to retrieve," type in Capman and hit the "Return" key. You will then bring in the unaltered Capman from the disk and your screen should show all the original numbers.

CUSTOMIZING THE MODEL

After you complete the exercises on the Capman file, you may wish to use AHI's financial model to plan your own company's capital requirements or to practice with a hypothetical company's figures.

Two Lotus 1-2-3 templates have been set up for this purpose.

1. CM.WKS is a blank financial model with the same relationships between financial assumptions and statements as the Noxton example you reviewed. In addition, this model gives you customizing capabilities of adding and deleting lines to the assumptions and individual statements.

2. CMNXTN.WKS has the same data as the Capman file and also has the customizing capabilities of the CM.WKS file. Since you are already familiar with the financial structure of the Noxton Manufacturing Company, use CMNXTN.WKS to step through the procedures of customizing a model. When you are comfortable in using these procedures, you can then load in the blank CM.WKS to set up your own financial model.

First, load CMNXTN.WKS. If you already have the Capman file

loaded, choose File from the Main Menu, and then Retrieve from the following menu. When the system prompts you for the name of the file you wish to load, type CMNXTN and hit "Return." If you do not have Capman loaded in, boot Lotus 1-2-3 and when you are in READY mode, type /FRCMNXTN and then hit "Return."

After CMNXTN has been loaded, you will see the Main Menu. You will notice that there is now an additional menu selection—number 6, Customize (Quit is now number 7). Now type the number 6. You will see the Customize Menu which includes all of the financial statements plus the assumptions.

You can now add a line to the Income Statement. Type the number 1 for Income Statement and then 1 again from the next menu to insert a line. The Lotus 1-2-3 Mode Indicator will read CMD READY and you will see the following message highlighted on your screen: "SCROLL TO LINE ABOVE WHICH YOU WISH TO INSERT A ROW, TYPE IN AN X, AND PRESS THE ENTER KEY TWICE."

The process of inserting or deleting a line is similar to entering a projection; you have the opportunity to move the cursor up and down a single column and to make an entry by typing a character within that column and then hitting the "Return" key twice. For this example, move the cursor to the line below Administrative Expenses, type an X, and hit the "Return" key twice. The system will place a "dummy" line in the Income Statement. This line will have X's for the line label and O's for the values of 19X5 through 19X9. The formulas representing this new line as a percentage of Sales for each of the five years will be in place. But the Customize function will only create the "form" of the new line of the financial statement. You must fill in its values and/or formulas for the actual and forecast years.

Now type M to return to the previous menu and type the number 7 for Work to move freely around the worksheet. Next, move to cell A136, type in the label for this line, General Expenses, and hit the "Return" key. Now move the cursor to D136 and type in 10 to represent $10,000 in General Expenses for 19X5. Next, move to F136 and type in 11 for the 19X6 figure. For the forecast years 19X7–19X9 you expect an increase in General Expenses of 15 percent over the previous year. You must now enter formulas to represent this increase. Move the cursor to I136. Type 1.15*F136 and hit "Return" (the F136 represents General Expenses for 19X6). Next, enter the formulas 1.15*I136 in cell K136 and 1.15*K136 in cell M136, to display figures for years 19X8 and 19X9, respectively. Next, press F9 to bring all calculations up-to-date.

Although you have completed entering the form and content of the new line in the income statement, there is one important step you must do before the customizing process is complete. You must move the cursor directly down to the total line closest to the newly inserted line and, if necessary, adjust the formula in this cell to reflect the presence of this line. For example, move the cursor to the Operating Income line cell for 19X5, D138. Note the formula (D133-(@SUM(D134. .D135))). An English translation of this mathematical representation is:

Operating Income = Gross Profit
                   − the sum of Selling and Administrative Expenses

Since you have added a new expenses line, you must adjust the Operating Income formula. Press the F2 key to get into Lotus 1-2-3's EDIT mode and change the formula to (D133-(@SUM(D134. .D136))).

Now add another line, this time in the Cash Flow Statement. You have three microcomputers each valued at $5,000. Cash Flow being what it is, you want to see what effect selling these items would have on your financial structure. It will be necessary to insert a line, Sale of Assets, in the Sources of Cash section.

Get back to the Main Menu by pressing Alt and M at the same time. Then type the numbers 6 and 3 to customize Cash Flow and 1 to insert a line. You will want to put this new line between Profit Before Taxes and Depreciation, so move the cursor to the Depreciation line, type in an X and press the "Return" key twice. The now familiar X's appear in the Sources of Cash. You now say, "Why sell these microcomputers?" You decide to forget the idea of selling the micros and delete the Sales of Assets line.

To do this, type 2 for Delete from the currently displayed menu. Then move the cursor to the XXXXXXXXX line, type an X and hit "Return" twice. The Cash Flow Statement should return to its original state.

Please note that if you insert a line, then change the affected total lines and then delete the inserted line, due to the vagaries of Lotus 1-2-3 you may get unexpected results in the form of ERR messages. We suggest that if you must delete an inserted line in a statement where total formulas have been changed, you bring in the original customizing template and reconstruct the statement from there.

When you are ready to create a model for your own company, load in the CM template. First enter the figures for the Actual years (by selecting Work off the Main Menu and then moving freely around the sheet). Get back into the Main Menu structure by typing Alt and M simultaneously.

SUMMARY OF CUSTOMIZING PROCEDURES

1. To insert a line in a statement, choose number 6, Customize, from the Main Menu. Then choose the number of the appropriate statement, type a 1 for Insert, move the cursor one line below where you wish to insert a row, type an X and hit "Return" twice.

2. Return to the Customize Menu by pressing M and then press 7 for Work to move freely around the sheet. When Lotus' Mode Indicator is set to READY, enter the label, values and/or formulas for the inserted line for all years.

3. Move down to the total line directly below the inserted row and, if necessary, adjust the formula to reflect the presence of the new line. Press the Alt and M keys simultaneously when finished to return to the menu structure.

4. In order to delete a previously inserted line, select number 6, Customize, from the Main Menu, and then choose 2 for Delete. Space down to the line you wish to delete, type an X and hit the "Return" key twice.

5. If you must delete an inserted line in a statement where total formulas have been changed, bring in the original customizing template and reconstruct the statement from there.

OTHER ASSUMPTIONS

There are a number of lines in the model whose formulas include assumptions which cannot be controlled by the user through entering different values in the Forecast Assumptions box. In your customized model, you may wish to go into these cells and edit the formulas to reflect your own assumptions.

Income Statement

Line 139, Interest Expense, has been given as the previous year's interest expense + 10 percent of the current year's new financing (for 19X7, +F139+(0.1 * F199). Depending on interest rates, you may want to adjust the 10 percent figure.

Line 144, Income Tax, is equal to 45 percent of current year's profit before tax (for 19X7, .45 * I141). You may want to use a different income tax rate.

Information for Cash Flow

Line 162, Other Payables, equals 3 percent of the sum of cost of sales, selling expense and administrative expense (for 19X7, .03*(I131 + I134+I135)). The 3 percent may or may not be adequate for your model.

Line 168, Depreciation, equals base year depreciation plus 10 percent of capital expenditures, cumulative for all years. You may wish to use a figure other than 10 percent.

Line 170, Taxes Paid, equals 25 percent of the income tax for the previous year plus 75 percent of the income tax for the current year (for 19X7, (F144*0.25)+(I144*0.750)). Your business may pay a greater or smaller percentage of each year's tax.

Balance Sheet

Income Tax Payable equals the previous year's Income Tax Payable plus 45 percent of the current year's profit before Tax Minus Taxes Paid (for 19X7, +D237+(0.45*I141)−F170)). See the discussion of line 144 in the Income Statement Section.

Index

discounted cash flow (DCF) rate of return,
80–83, 94–96
for capital investments, 93
for equipment replacement, 102–104
of incremental cash flow, 100
multiple, for some capital investments,
104–105
for projects, 87–88
ranking capital projects by, 105
for warehouse investment, 104
worksheet for, 84–85
dividend growth model, for cost of common
capital, 66–67
dividends, and free cash flow, 20
division managers, establishing return on
investment standards for, 74
divisions,
capital allocation to, 114–115
profit goals, 114
Dow-Jones Industrial Stocks, 62–63

earning yield approach, to cost of common
capital calculation, 66
earnings ratios, 27
economy, capital use decisions effect on, 1
equipment,
after-tax cost of purchase, 58
age and book rates of return, 83
leasing costs, 53–55
repair vs replacement, 100–102
replacement and discounted cash flow rate
of return, 102–104
residual value of leased, 56
useful life of, 17
expansion, capital expenditures for, 91

File option, in Capman Main Menu, 124
files description, for Capman model, 121–122
finance,
aspects of, 2
relation to control/accounting, 2–3
financial management, objectives of, 4–5
financial manager,
responsibility of, 6
role of, 4
senior, 2
financial model,
assumptions, 133–134
customizing, 130–133
financial ratios, see ratios
financial reporting, recommendations from
ratio analysis, 46
financial statements, see also balance sheet;
cash flow statement; income statement

accountant responsibility for, 9
reviewing in Capman, 126–128
fixed capital,
analysis of, 15–16
in balance sheet analysis, 16
relation to working capital, 15
fixed costs, 79
foreign business ventures, and risk, 86
formulas, entry on spreadsheet, 131–132
free cash flow,
calculation, 19–20
defined, 19
projected, 113

goals, long-term, 106
growth rate approach, to cost of capital
calculation, 64
growth rate impact, and Capman model, 128
growth ratios, 33–35
worksheet for, 34

income statement, 6, 119
analysis of, 9–13
model assumptions, 134
projected, 111
income to capital ratio, 27
income to sales ratio, 27
incremental cash flow, discounted cash flow
rate of return of, 100
industrial bonds, yield to maturity, 50, 52
insertion of lines, in spreadsheet, 131, 133
interest cost, analysis of effective, 50, 51
internal rate of return, 80
inventory,
analysis of, 23–24
growth and cash flow statement, 19
increases in balance sheet analysis, 16
inventory to working capital ratio, 41, 42
investment, return on, see return on
investment, 70–88

lease amortization schedule, 57
leases,
after-tax cost of, 56, 58–59
calculating true cost of, 53–55
and cash flow projections, 112
cost compared to purchasing with debt,
55–59
long-term capital, 16
lenders,
long-term, and capital ratio analysis,
43–46
short-term, ratio analysis of concern to,
40–43

ANSWER TO CAPITAL PLANNING PROBLEM:

To meet the financial objectives of management, cost of sales cannot exceed 80 percent of sales, and inventory cannot exceed 33 percent of cost of sales during the forecast period. In addition, Noxton's dividend payout ratio must be reduced from 60 percent to no more than 54 percent each year of the forecast.